WIT

Saving Private Ryan

Adapted from the novel by
MAX ALLAN COLLINS
Based on the screenplay by
ROBERT RODAT

Level 6

Retold by Jacqueline Kehl
Series Editors: Andy Hopkins and Jocelyn Potter

Pearson Education Limited
Edinburgh Gate, Harlow,
Essex CM20 2JE, England
and Associated Companies throughout the world.

ISBN 978-0-582-41983-4

First published in the USA by Penguin Putnam Inc. 1998
First published in Great Britain by Penguin Books 1998
This edition first published 2000

10

TM & © 1998, 2000 Paramount Pictures, Dream Works LLC and
Amblin Entertainment

Typeset by Digital Type, London
Set in 11/14pt Bembo
Printed in China
SWTC/10

Published by Pearson Education Limited in association with
Penguin Books Ltd, both companies being subsidiaries of Pearson Plc

Contents

Introduction

*Boys became men as they crossed the killing zone of Omaha Beach—
often dead men, but men. Running, shouting, screaming, crawling on
hands and knees, they moved toward the sea wall. Men whose rifles had
sand in them, or who had lost their weapons in the water, grabbed guns
from the dead. Shell holes provided temporary shelter; a tank provided
cover. As some men were hit, other soldiers picked up the wounded and
carried them. Others could not be helped. The sound of wounded and
dying men filled the air: "Mama! Mother! Mom!"*

Thousands of kilometers from this Normandy beach, a mother in
Iowa will soon receive terrible news. Three of her four sons are
dead, victims of the war. The Pentagon comes to a quick
decision. The fourth brother must come home safely, if it is not
too late. The task of bringing him from the killing fields is given
to Captain Miller and his men. But can they save him? And can
they save themselves? This is a story of the real horrors of war, but
also of courage and self-discovery.

Praised by audiences and reviewers around the world, Steven
Spielberg's *Saving Private Ryan* is an unforgettable film
achievement. The novel based on the movie was written by Max
Allan Collins. He has written thrillers, film criticism, short
fiction, songs, and other novels from movies and TV series,
including *In the Line of Fire*, *Waterworld*, and *Air Force One*. Collins
has also written, directed, and produced independent films.

Chapter 1   A Family Visit

The pathway was lined with hedges high enough to block everything else from view. Grandpa walked quickly ahead of the others through the tunnel of green. Jimmy, the youngest of the two brothers and two sisters, could hardly stay with him. He couldn't believe that an old man like Grandpa could move so fast. Mom, Dad, and the rest of the family were almost running to keep up with him.

Suddenly Grandpa stopped. He fell to his knees.

"Dad!" Mom called from behind Jimmy, and her voice was full of concern.

But Jimmy knew now that Grandpa hadn't fallen; he was . . . kneeling. Praying.

Soon Jimmy knew why. When he came up beside his grandfather, who was staring at the landscape at the end of the path, Jimmy saw an amazing design. It had surely been created by both God and man: the green grass was God's work, and the sea of white crosses was man's.

Jimmy, who was seven, had seen only one other cemetery, and it was much smaller. This one looked like everybody on earth had died and been buried here. As far as he could see, there was only green, white, green, white, green, white.

Then Mom and Dad ran to Grandpa, put their arms around him, and held him tightly; Jimmy's brothers and sisters were coming, too, and finally his grandmother. There was an odd expression on her face; Jimmy couldn't tell whether she was happy or sad.

1

Grandpa's face had no expression at all. His eyes were open wide as he stared at the crosses. Those eyes must have seen a lot of things in all those years, Jimmy thought.

The boy wondered if Grandpa was thinking about people who were buried in this place—people who had been his friends. Dad said Grandpa had fought in the war here, but Jimmy didn't understand—not really. He had heard of that war in Vietnam. But this was France.

Maybe a war was fought here, once, too.

Chapter 2   On the Landing Boat

A gray sea met the gray sky, but the 5,000 ships in shades of darker gray moved forward. Nothing could stop the transport ships as they moved across the English Channel in ten lines, thirty kilometers across.

These ships, however, were not making the assault on the beaches of Normandy. Fifteen hundred landing boats, which would make the twenty-kilometer trip from the bigger ships to the beach in three and a half endless hours, were making the assault. The first group of landing boats consisted of 200 boats– larger ones carrying 200 men each, and smaller ones carrying thirty men, or twelve men plus a jeep.

In one of the smaller boats Captain John H. Miller—from Addley, Pennsylvania—sat with his men, who had just finished their training. At thirty-eight years old, he was the oldest man on the boat. His hand was shaking, and he hoped his boys hadn't seen it. He stared at it, trying to stop the trembling, forcing the fear back inside him—and the hand obeyed.

None of his boys had noticed their captain's trembling hand; they were busy watching their boat push on through the waves. The freezing water blew in, wetting all their clothes and filling the boat. The boat, battling the waves, threw the soldiers around. They wore life jackets and helmets and carried a variety of weapons. Many used their helmets to throw the water out of the boat.

A lot of the boys were seasick. Some stood bent over the side of the boat. Private Anthony Caparzo—twenty-two, Chicago,

Illinois—had collected a lot of pills for seasickness on the transport ship and had planned to sell them when they were needed. But now, seeing his sick friends, he just gave them away.

Stanley Mellish—twenty-one, Yonkers, New York— grabbed a handful of pills.

"Give me some of those!" he said.

"That's my entire wartime supply."

"What difference does it make?" Mellish responded. "Do you really think we're going to be taking anymore boat rides after this?"

Caparzo had no answer. More huge waves came and lifted the boat out of the water. The boys were either being sick or praying.

Miller stood at the side of the boat, watching his boys. Next to him was Sergeant Michael Horvath—thirty, Minneapolis, Minnesota. Sarge gestured to the sick and praying soldiers.

"I guess they don't do much boating back home," he said.

Miller loved these kids. One of the boys, Danny Delancey, was a sweet kid who was a good singer. Right now he was looking over the side of the boat.

"Heads down!" Miller shouted. "There's nothing to see!"

But before Delancey could obey that order, the boat next to theirs ran into a mine, causing a huge explosion. Delancey fell back as everyone on the boat was hit with flaming oil, burned body parts, and small pieces of metal. They used their helmets to pour water on the flames.

They cursed and screamed in horror as they cleaned the boat. Miller threw a foot in a boot overboard, and Sarge threw a burned arm. The two men glanced at each other, and the youthful faces around them turned toward their leaders for guidance.

"Injuries?" Miller called out.

All shook their heads, no, which was amazing. Faces were turning toward the water, where bodies—and body parts— floated.

"Heads down, I said!"

"Captain"—Delancey's eyes were open wide—"are we all going to die?"

Miller was trying to think of the right words—he didn't want to be dishonest with these boys, but they needed something hopeful to take with them into battle—when Lieutenant Frank Briggs responded for him.

"No, Delancey!" Briggs said, trying to sound cheerful. "Two-thirds, at the most!"

Those weren't the kind of words that Miller had hoped for.

"Oh, God," Delancey said. The line between curses and prayers was unclear in the war.

Briggs—thirty, Dallas, Texas—put his hands around his mouth and shouted loudly, "Look at the man on your left! All of you. Now look at the man on your right!"

All around the boat, the boys obeyed.

Briggs grinned. "Say a prayer for those two boys, because they're not coming back. You, on the other hand, aren't going to get a scratch!"

Delancey smiled weakly. Briggs's words had clearly made the men more uncomfortable than ever.

The sky filled with orange-white light, and all eyes looked up. Thousands of rockets flashed overhead, followed by thunderous explosions.

"See that?" Miller shouted. "Hear that? That's the sight and sound of Germans dying!"

"Go, Americans!" Lieutenant Briggs called out.

"Now, get those heads back down," Miller said, as he looked at the mist-covered shoreline. He could see rows of steel crosses and wooden logs with mines on top of them, all angled toward the sea. The Germans had put them on the beach to tear apart landing boats at high tide when the water made them invisible. At low tide they provided cover for foot soldiers moving across the beach.

Miller was surprised to see these still in place. He had been told that they would be removed before dawn. But there they were—steel crosses, like grave markers in a cemetery that was waiting to be filled. The American bombing, it seemed to Miller, was failing. He had hoped the beach would be full of shell holes, as promised. That was how he had trained his men—moving in and out and around shell holes . . .

"It's going to be a big show!" one kid shouted.

Nearby, Daniel Boone Jackson—twenty-three, Hickory Valley, Tennessee—held his sharpshooter's rifle tightly and bowed his head.

"It's time to make your peace with God," Jackson advised his friends.

Suddenly the waves grew calmer and the waters became quiet. The bombing had stopped, leaving only the sound of the boat engines—a sound so familiar to these passengers that they no longer noticed it. It seemed the war had halted to give these boys the moment of silence that they needed.

Miller knew this minute of accidental quiet was the only break his kids were likely to have on this cold, gray morning. He glanced at the boatman, who held up three fingers. His boys were looking at him. They knew this was the signal to leave the boat; they needed only their final orders.

Miller seldom made speeches, so he glanced at the sergeant, and they smiled at each other—tiny smiles that might be a final goodbye. Then the captain moved among his boys, keeping his manner and his voice conversational and calm.

"Keep it simple," he said softly, "move fast, stay apart . . . Good luck."

Occasionally he gave a small smile or a pat on a shoulder.

"Don't get any sand in your rifles," he said. "Good luck, men."

The Navy's big guns started shooting again, but at the same time enemy shooting and mortar fire rained down on the approaching landing boats. The sound of machine guns came from both sides, and Miller saw bullets hitting the water and the sides of the boat just a little ahead of them. He knew that for every bullet you saw, there were four more bullets that you didn't. Then the boat moved forward, ran onto the sand, and stopped.

"It looks like there's a little opposition," Mellish said.

As the men stared straight ahead, another shower of bullets began. Miller realized that he had two choices: he could send his men directly into the machine-gun fire, or they could stay in the boat until mortar fire or an artillery shell killed them all.

The machine-gun fire stopped occasionally. Miller decided to move during one of the breaks. As he was thinking, the boys who were his men backed away from the bullets as well as they could in the crowded boat.

"I'm so seasick," said one kid. "I wish I was off this boat."

Miller shouted to his boys: "When I say 'Now,' I want you to get off fast! Understood? ... See you on the beach! Good luck!"

Every boy on the boat was saying to himself: *"It can't happen to me ... can it?"*

Then the machine-gun fire stopped. The gate in the side of the boat opened, and Miller shouted, "Now!" The men ran through the opening and jumped off the boat.

And the machine-gun fire started again.

Miller heard the sounds of machine-gun fire and of his boys screaming as they died. He could only see their backs, as the heavy bullets blew them apart.

Although Miller had been in many battles, he was not prepared for this. In less than twenty seconds, two-thirds of his men were killed. The water was full of dead and dying soldiers, and the survivors were splashing around among them with fear in their eyes.

"Go! Go!" Miller shouted loudly enough to be heard above the machine-gun storm.

Still on the boat, Private Delancey was screaming. It was a scream of horror; he was caught under a pile of dead bodies. Miller, staying low, pulled the boy from the pile just a moment before the machine-gun fire reached it. Then he dragged Delancey to the open gate and, still holding onto him, jumped into the deep water.

Chapter 3   Landing

Miller's three-kilo backpack, full of equipment, sank him like a rock, and he went down through the drowning soldiers. Men were dropping their equipment to survive, and filling the underwater world with helmets, rifles, and mortar. Seeing this, Miller was determined to hold onto his rifle while he took off his backpack.

When his backpack was off, Miller realized that the soldier floating nearest him was Private Delancey, who couldn't remove his own heavy pack. Miller assisted, releasing the pack to join the rest of the abandoned equipment falling to the sandy floor.

But the kid was scared now. Air bubbles were coming out of his open, silently screaming mouth, and his eyes were wide with fear. The captain put an arm tightly around the private and swam with him, underwater, staying below the shooting.

Soon the captain and private were above the surface again. They breathed in air as their ears filled with the sounds of Omaha Beach: shells exploding, men screaming, gunfire, machine-gun bullets hitting the sand.

Delancey held onto Miller tightly. The captain carried him through the shallow water, bullets splashing around them. Other soldiers walked the same path—many without helmets or weapons. These exhausted survivors arrived on the beach.

Miller carried Delancey around the steel crosses, and then

stopped behind one of them to rest for a moment. Suddenly machine-gun fire hit Delancey's back, killing him at once. The captain could do nothing to help his private now, so he used the body to protect himself. Walking toward shore, Miller felt Delancey's body being hit again and again. He wondered if this might finally be the moment he would go crazy.

Exhausted, he paused beneath the bloody body of the boy that he had tried to save and looked around. He saw that he was not alone: hundreds of men from other boats were walking toward the shore—finding their way through the dead bodies in the water.

The captain threw himself behind another steel cross, just as machine-gun fire hammered the metal. Suddenly an artillery shell exploded just behind him, throwing him into the water.

Seconds later he got up. He looked into the water and saw a helmet floating. It was his. He put it on and looked at his face in the water. It wasn't a captain's face or a soldier's; it was the face of a man ready to die. His uniform was torn; his skin was scratched and bleeding. He wondered why the shooting had stopped; was the battle over?

The world was silent. Hundreds of dead soldiers covered the beach. Others, wounded, moved around in pain and fear. Miller saw their mouths moving. Some were crying silently for help or for their mothers; others were screaming. But there was no sound.

He looked around. The sand was covered with rifles, helmets, and blankets. Some men had arrived on the beach, and were shooting toward the enemy hidden in the cliffs on both sides of them.

Suddenly he was staring into the face of a private, a blue-eyed boy who looked at him strangely. Nearby three more privates were sitting behind a steel cross, shivering in the cold water. They were looking at him strangely, too.

Miller was confused. "What?"

The blue-eyed private's mouth moved. Miller realized that his confusion and loss of hearing were caused by the artillery shell that had exploded behind him.

"Did you say something, soldier?" Miller said.

The private said, "What now, sir?" but Miller only saw his lips moving.

"*What?*" Miller screamed, unaware that he was screaming. "*What are you saying?*"

"*I said,*" the private screamed back at the captain, "*what do we do now, sir?*"

Miller glanced around. He forced himself to look past the dead bodies and realized that he was not alone. Many others were alive and were taking cover behind the steel crosses.

"*Captain! Captain!*" He heard the familiar voice just as his hearing returned. On the other side of him, Miller could see Sergeant Michael Horvath, who was sitting behind another steel cross; from Sarge's expression, Miller understood that the man had been shouting at him for a long time.

Miller let himself smile briefly, happy that his friend was still alive. Then, in a voice that was all business, he said, "Get these men off the beach."

One of the group of young privates asked, "Sir, where will we meet?"

Miller pointed toward the cliffs, a distance of about two hundred meters. "Get there and they can't shoot you!"

Beyond the steel crosses, the body-covered beach sloped gently upward to a stone sea wall. At some places along the beach, the sea wall was four or five meters high—but here it was only about one. The top of the wall was covered with wire. Groups of soldiers were already sitting against it, using it for cover to avoid the machine-gun and rifle fire coming from the cliffs. They were digging holes and taking care of the wounded.

"The sea wall!" Miller shouted to the twenty or thirty privates hiding behind the steel crosses in the shallow water. "Do you see it?"

A frightened soldier's voice cried out: "I'm staying here!"

"Get off this beach!" Miller shouted, above the gunfire. "If you stay here, the machine guns or an artillery shell will get you. And the tide is rising, every minute! That sea wall is life . . . you're all dead here!"

Miller ran out from behind the steel cross, his rifle ready. He ran through the shallow water and around the dead men. Dozens joined him—suddenly soldiers again.

Boys became men as they crossed the killing zone of Omaha Beach—often dead men, but men. Running, shouting, screaming, crawling on hands and knees, they moved toward the sea wall. Men whose rifles had sand in them, or who had lost their weapons in the water, grabbed guns from the dead. Shell holes provided temporary shelter; a tank provided cover. As some men were hit, other soldiers picked up the wounded and carried them. Others could not be helped. The sound of wounded and dying men filled the air: "Mama! Mother! Mom!"

"Help me out of here," a voice said.

Behind a steel cross Lieutenant Frank Briggs lay in the sand. He was wounded. Miller picked him up, and they went on through the bullets toward the sea wall. He suddenly felt stronger. But he wasn't; Briggs was lighter—the lower half of the lieutenant was gone.

Then someone ran into him: Sarge. The sergeant grabbed him and pulled him along. They walked the last twelve meters through a shower of bullets and threw themselves to the ground along the edge of the sea wall. Miller had never been so exhausted. His eyes hurt, and every bone in his body ached.

Up and down the beach, other brave, lucky, exhausted soldiers reached the safety of the sea wall. Still, the machine-gun and mortar fire continued, and the casualties increased.

"I can't tell the dead from the wounded," Miller said.

Along the sea wall, soldiers turned their faces toward Miller. They had made men of themselves, crossing that bloody beach. But now they were boys again, and in the safety of the shelter they allowed their fear to show.

Miller looked at these scared kids, some crying. "Who's in command up here?" he asked.

There were two answers to that question: machine-gun fire from above said that the Germans were in command. But several of the young privates shouted the other answer: "You are! You are, sir!"

Miller looked at Sarge. "I was afraid of that," he whispered.

"Don't get killed," Sarge whispered back, "or I'll be in command."

"We don't want that," Miller said, smiling. "Do you recognize where we are?"

"About two kilometers from where we're supposed to be?"

Hearing this, a soldier down the sea wall called out, "Nobody's where they're supposed to be!"

A private next to Sarge added, "He's right, sir, we're all mixed up."

Miller surveyed this mix of men from different companies. Knowing that their sea-wall shelter was only a temporary stop, he repeated to himself, "*I was afraid of that.*"

Chapter 4   On the Beach

Miller and Sarge walked along the sea wall, looking for their men. Private Robert Reiben—twenty-four, Brooklyn, New York—raced in from the beach and threw himself against the sea wall between his captain and sergeant.

Sarge asked him, "Have you seen anybody else from the company?"

"Jackson," Reiben said. The sharpshooter, his rifle in his hand, had reached the wall. "But that's all."

"Mellish, here, sir!" a voice called from the other direction.

"Caparzo, too, sir!" another voice called from the same direction.

Miller leaned out just far enough to see them; then he pulled back as Caparzo's voice continued: "Wade's back there with DeForest."

"Where *is* Wade?" Miller called back.

"Out there on the beach," Caparzo shouted, "trying to save DeForest."

Finally Miller saw the company medic, Corporal Edward Wade—San Diego, California, at twenty-eight one of the oldest of the captain's boys. He was kneeling over Private Brian DeForest—twenty-one, DeKalb, Illinois—trying to save him, even though he had a huge chest wound. Wade was bloody up to his elbows. He ignored a senior medical officer's orders to move onto the next wounded soldier, insisting, "He's not gone, sir." As men dropped around him in the killing zone, Wade calmly piled the dead bodies to give him cover. Then he continued working on his friend.

"Wade!" Miller called from the sea wall. "Wade! *Wade!*"

But Wade didn't hear—or maybe ignored—his captain.

Miller shouted, "Mellish—Caparzo ... get Wade off that beach! We're *not* losing our medic!"

Machine-gun fire hit the piled bodies, but Wade kept working on his friend. Then a bullet passed through one of the bodies and hit DeForest in the side of the head, killing him.

Just then Caparzo and Mellish reached Wade. They dragged him off the beach to the sea wall.

Miller turned to Sarge. "That's it? That's all of us?"

"Maybe not, sir. We got separated. There are probably more of us somewhere around here."

"Not enough. Not enough." He was thinking of the landing boat and how he had sent his boys out into the machine-gun fire. But the sound of mortars reminded him that there wasn't time for thinking.

"Where's our exit?" he asked Sarge.

"The gap in the cliffs on the right."

"Gather weapons!" Miller announced. "Whatever you have, whatever you can find! Drag them in off the sand if you have to! Those weapons aren't doing anybody any good out there!"

His order was passed up and down the sea wall. The men seemed excited by the idea of taking action. They were tired of sitting along the sea wall, waiting for bullets or an exploding mortar to get them. They went out to the beach and picked up all the guns, rifles, and other weapons they could find.

Miller looked at the wire on top of the sea wall. "We'll need pipe bombs to blow a hole in that and explode any mines in the ground nearby," he said. "Where are the engineers?"

The men returned with their weapons and gathered around the captain and sergeant.

"I'm impressed," Miller admitted with a tiny smile.

Two engineer sergeants arrived and began pushing explosives into pipes and laying them in a line along the beach to the top of the sea wall. Others began cleaning the sand out of weapons and checking that they worked. Miller saw Mellish and Caparzo grinning as they cleaned a newly acquired machine gun. Most of the men were strangers to Miller, but he loved them as much as the two children waiting for him at home.

While Miller watched the men, Wade came up beside him. "Good to see you, sir," Wade said quietly.

"Good to be seen," Miller admitted, glad that Wade had joined them again.

One of the engineers signaled: the explosive-stuffed pipe line was ready. "Fire!" Sarge shouted, and the soldiers took cover. The explosion was just one more noise. When the smoke and dust cleared, a wide gap in the wire provided an exit from the bloody beach.

"All right!" Sarge shouted. "Let's go through that hole!"

Miller lifted himself up the sea wall and crawled through the gap. A dozen men—including Reiben, Mellish, Caparzo, Wade, and Sarge—were right behind him. They raced to the beach area beyond, where there were patches of high grass and trenches.

But the fire of the German machine guns changed direction to follow the runners and to stop others from coming through the gap in the wire. Three men were killed. This discouraged some, but others ran forward, following Miller and his men.

As they started up the slope, staying in the cover of the trenches, the machine gun fire stopped. It was strangely silent. The soldiers divided into little groups, keeping low, and went up the hill.

A group of five soldiers in the trench ahead of Reiben had stopped before a turn they couldn't see around; then they looked at each other and went around the corner anyway. The firing began again, and two of the men hurried back. The rest of the group stopped and watched as German grenades came from around the bend.

"*This* way! *This* way!" Miller called.

Miller ran up a deep trench, and the others followed his confident lead. Ahead of Miller, three privates went around a corner. Suddenly the thunder of exploding land mines warned Miller to stop. He looked around the corner and saw that two of the soldiers were dead and the third stood motionless, trapped in a mine field.

Then came an unexpected sound: whistling, human whistling that sounded like someone calling a pet. A voice followed, "Fritz! Fritz!" It was a German voice.

Soon a dog ran through the passage behind them, surprising

Miller and his men. They grinned as the dog passed them. The animal took a pathway away from the trench, and Miller saw a gray-coated, helmeted man run from behind a turn in the path. The man took the barking dog into his arms and pulled the animal to safety—around the corner, out of sight.

Miller thought about the soldier who loved his dog. But this thought was interrupted when the German soldier reappeared. He aimed his rifle, and shot the trapped American in the head.

Then the German was gone.

Miller paused on the path, but no one commented on the killing. Some things are too terrible to mention, and they knew that, in the German's place, they might have done the same.

"We're dead!" a boy behind him said in a frightened voice. "All the exits are mined!"

Sarge quietly said to Miller, "It wasn't easy getting here, sir, but getting out's going to be even harder."

Miller turned and smiled at his boys—a smile that he hoped looked confident—and said, "That dog, Fritz, knew the way out."

Mellish, chewing gum nervously, said, "Do you think that dog knows where the mines are?"

"That dog is with the German personnel," Miller said, "and they travel up and down these trenches every day, don't they?"

Then Miller ran up the pathway Fritz had taken. His men followed him. They had gone a good distance up the sloping trench when their captain raised his hand for them to halt.

The pathway was rising to a gap in the walls at the end of the trench. The soldiers could see across the slope to a rock pile about ten meters ahead. It looked good. But the sound of machine guns and rifles shooting at the beach had increased in volume, and the sound of mortars was close, too. Running across that gap might put Miller and his men in sight of the Germans.

"We're at a bad angle; we can't see what's ahead," Sarge said as the group gathered within the walls of the trench. "We won't know what's up there until we put our heads out."

"Who has a mirror?" Miller asked, and one was passed to him.

He looked at Mellish and said, "Give me your gum."

He took the gum, put it on the tip of his rifle, and stuck the mirror to the gum. Then, as his men grinned and nodded around him, the captain held the rifle out, just enough to get a view. He saw a cliff overlooking the beach about twenty meters beyond their position, but it was between their trench and the protective rock pile. On the cliff, seven meters above them, were two machine-gun teams, shooting down at the beach. Other Germans were throwing mortars, and another small group of soldiers was guarding the position. Pulling the mirror back in, Miller reported to his men.

Sarge nodded toward the rock pile. "There's our perfect firing position, but it's not going to be easy to get there."

"Let's get ready to go," Miller said. He turned to the four soldiers nearest him and nodded to each.

"When they go, we'll shoot to cover them. It'll get the Germans' attention and keep them busy."

All nodded.

"Those machine guns are heavy," Miller told the four boys. "The Germans won't be able to move them around quickly. The soldiers up there will shoot at you. Run left and right, not in a straight line. Stay apart. Understand?"

Four young faces looked at him and nodded.

"Then go!"

The four boys raced into the open area. Miller and the others sent a storm of bullets toward the German position. Shots were returned, but they weren't directed at the trench. That could only mean that the Germans were firing down on the open area where the boys had run.

When the shooting stopped, Miller called out, "Report in!"

Silence.

The captain ran out for a quick look. The bodies of the four boys were on the ground. Miller dove back, as rifle shots narrowly missed him.

Miller looked at the men who remained and selected three more boys. Sarge looked at him with an expression that showed Miller the craziness of what they were doing. He stopped and considered his options for a moment. Then he said to sharpshooter Jackson, "Are you ready to go across?"

"I'm ready, sir."

Miller ran into the open area and stood there, making a perfect target. Up on the cliff, one of the machine-gun teams began turning their heavy weapon.

"Go!" Miller shouted.

Jackson ran through the open space as the machine-gun fire turned toward Miller. The captain dove back into the trench, as machine-gun bullets took the heel off his boot. Jackson was running left and right, avoiding the bullets as he neared the rock pile.

Miller called out: "Report!"

Jackson's voice replied: "Here!"

The men in the trench smiled. Suddenly machine-gun fire started again, and the men threw themselves down and screamed. But Miller knew that Jackson would not be discouraged.

Jackson had his rifle aimed at a German machine gunner and was softly praying.

The captain called, "Jackson—do you have a shot?"

Jackson called back, "Send over a group!"

The sharpshooter shot, and the German machine gun stopped firing. A bullet had gone through the machine gunner's head.

Down in the trench, Sarge was saying, "We can do it!"

Groups of Americans raced across the open area to the rock pile. Then everybody joined in Miller's wild cry as he led his boys out from behind the rock pile and up the steep slope.

The battle was fierce and short. Miller and his boys took the German position. A few Americans were killed, but all of the Germans went down.

"To their bunker!" Miller shouted.

Machine-gun and rifle fire came from the bunker as the boys raced to it. Two boys went down, but the rest were too fast to get hit.

"Grenades," Miller said. They threw their grenades through the opening in the bunker. The boys fell and covered themselves as fire from the bunker followed.

"Let them have it!" Miller shouted, getting to his feet. He shot through the opening, and his boys did, too.

When the shooting was over, Miller walked across the blackened cliff. He was alive. He had never expected to get off the beach.

They all shared this feeling, but no one spoke. There were no words to express what they felt. They were here, and they were alive. That was enough.

Miller joined the sergeant, who was standing at the edge of the cliff.

"What a view," Sarge said.

On the horizon an endless row of ships watched silently as landing boat after landing boat pushed through the dead bodies, moving toward the beach. Seasick soldiers ran through the shallow water onto the sand. They took cover behind the steel crosses and then ran through the smoke and fallen bodies toward the safety of the sea wall.

Shells continued to explode in the water and on shore. But still the American soldiers came. Nothing could stop their advance.

It was a terrible landscape of horror and death. And a magnificent statement about the courage of the men fighting and dying there.

"What a view," Miller agreed.

Helmets, damaged radios, wire, weapons, and bodies lay on the sand. Written on the backpack of one of the dead soldiers was a last name: RYAN.

But, of course, from where he stood, Miller couldn't see that.

Chapter 5   A Problem

Inside the Pentagon, the year-and-a-half old, five-sided building that was the largest office building in the world, another group fought the war in a different manner. The sounds were those of typewriters, not machine guns; and the room was full of desks, not trenches.

The secretaries served their country by typing the words: "We regret to inform you ... killed in action ... heroic service ..." These men and women were writing messages that would sadden mothers, fathers, brothers and sisters, sons and daughters all around the country.

Typing the same words again and again was sometimes boring. When Lucy Freemont placed a sheet of paper on the growing pile of finished work on her desk, the name "RYAN" did not disturb her routine. She had started typing a second sheet before a second word—"IOWA"—reminded her of something, and she frowned.

Lucy wasn't bored as she went through her pile, looking for a message that she had typed more than an hour ago. Then she looked through the files to check again. The other workers watched her as she rose quickly from her desk and hurried from the room.

The news passed quickly from Lucy Freemont to her lieutenant to his captain. All were disturbed by what she had discovered. Lucy was back in her office when Captain John McRae—twenty-eight, Peoria, Illinois—took the news to his superior officer.

Colonel Wilson—forty-seven, Atlanta, Georgia—was in a war room. The walls were covered with maps of Normandy, and the maps had pins in them showing American positions. Wilson was pouring a cup of coffee when Captain McRae approached him.

"Colonel," the captain said, "we've just learned something you should know about."

Wilson saw the three sheets of paper that the captain was holding. "Well, what is it, Captain?"

"You should read it yourself, sir."

The captain handed him two of the sheets of paper. Wilson glanced at them and saw that the words "RYAN" and "IOWA" were on both of them. He sat down at his desk as the captain spoke again.

"These two men died in Normandy," McRae began. "One at Omaha Beach, the other at Utah Beach."

"I can see that," Wilson said, reading the death messages. "Thomas Ryan. Peter Ryan. Brothers?"

"Yes, sir. And this man . . ." He handed Wilson a third sheet of paper. ". . . This man was killed last week in New Guinea."

"Daniel Ryan," the colonel said. The word "IOWA" appeared again. "Oh God . . . Brothers? Three brothers, all killed in action?"

"Yes, sir. And I've just learned that this afternoon their mother will be receiving all three messages."

The colonel's face became pale. "Oh, God," he said, almost shouting. The room was quiet. Everyone—the other officers, the secretaries—had stopped working when they heard him.

"There's a fourth brother in Normandy, sir."

Wilson frowned. "I don't see a fourth death message . . ."

"No, at least not yet, sir. The fourth brother, James—he's the youngest, sir—parachuted in with the 101st Airborne the night before the landing."

"Well, where is he now?"

"We don't know, sir. Somewhere in Normandy, we assume."

"Is he alive?" Wilson asked.

"We don't know that, either, sir."

Wilson covered his eyes with his hand, leaning on his elbow. His team around him couldn't tell whether he was thinking or praying, but they gave him the respectful silence he required. After a moment he shouted, "Get back to work." He stood up, nodding to McRae, and ordered, "Come with me."

♦

As the colonel and captain in Washington, DC, left the war room, a black government car was on its way to the Ryan farmhouse in Iowa. In the window of the house a flag with four blue stars—one for every member of the family in the military—was proudly displayed.

Margaret Ryan—sixty—was alone on the farm. When she heard the approaching car, she stepped onto the porch. Seeing the car approach her house made her uncomfortable, but the lane was shared by four farms. They might not stop here.

But they did. As the three men got out of the car, she fell against a post of the porch, holding it tightly. She began to cry, knowing that she had lost one of her boys—never imagining that this terrible news could be much, much worse.

♦

At the same time, in the Pentagon, the Army Chief of Staff, General Marshall, was meeting with Colonel Wilson, Captain McRae, and the general's assistant, Colonel Louis Dye. They were standing at a large table reading the files on the Ryan brothers.

General Marshall—sixty-four—threw the files on the table and demanded, "How did we let this happen, after the Sullivans?"

McRae responded, "Originally, all four of them were in the same company, but we separated them after the Sullivans."

23

The five Sullivan brothers of Waterloo, Iowa, had all served on the same ship, which was bombed off Guadalcanal in November 1942. The tragedy had made the public extremely angry.

"Sir," Colonel Dye offered, "the army doesn't officially separate or protect brothers. The Navy made that rule, and besides, these Ryans weren't serving together . . ."

"Would you like to be the one who informs the War Department Office of Public Relations of this?" Marshall shouted.

"No," Dye admitted.

"Do we have any contact with the fourth brother . . . what's the boy's name?" Marshall asked.

"James," Wilson said. "No, sir. He was dropped with the paratroopers about twenty-five kilometers from the coast—near Neuville."

"And that's behind German lines, isn't it?"

"Yes, sir."

"We can't be sure, sir," Dye added. "The first reports said the 101st got separated. They were dropped in the wrong places all over Normandy. We had a high casualty rate, too. Ryan may not even have survived the jump. Even if he did, he was probably killed in action."

Marshall said nothing; his face was serious. He moved to his desk and called his secretary. "Captain Newsome, bring me the Bixby file, please."

"Yes, General," a female voice replied.

"Private Ryan could be anywhere, sir," Dye started again. "If we send a squad through German territory, we'll be sending out death messages to all of *their* mothers."

Marshall shook his head and sighed. Captain Florence Newsome, his personal secretary, entered and handed him a file. He thanked her, and she left.

The general moved slowly to his desk, sat down, and withdrew an old sheet of paper. "I have a letter here, written some time ago, to a Mrs. Bixby in Boston." He put on his reading glasses.

" 'Dear Mrs. Bixby,' " he read. " 'I have been shown in the files of the War Department a statement that you are the mother of five sons who have died honorably on the field of battle. My words can't take away the grief of such a loss. But I feel I must write to offer you the thanks of the Republic they have died to save.' "

Marshall put the piece of paper on top of the file on his desk. But he wasn't finished.

" 'I pray that our Heavenly Father may lessen your sadness,' " he continued from memory, " 'and leave you only the wonderful memory of your sons and the pride that you should have in such a great gift to your country.' " He paused and then continued, "And it's signed: 'Yours very sincerely and respectfully, Abraham Lincoln.' "

The captain and the colonel glanced at each other. This letter had been written in a different war—over a hundred years ago—but they were not surprised at how strongly the general felt.

Marshall's eyes were determined as he said, "If that boy is alive, we're going to send somebody to find him and get him out of there."

Chapter 6   The Mission

As a line of jeeps, tanks, and other vehicles moved along nearby, Captain John Miller sat in the shelter of an artillery-shell hole with the men from his company who were still alive—Privates Reiben, Caparzo, Mellish, Jackson; Sergeant Horvath; and company-medic Wade. They were enjoying a few minutes of rest and relaxation after lunch. Miller thought his men looked older.

"Do you think it's true," Reiben asked the others, "that the Japanese do terrible things to their prisoners?"

"That's not our war," Sarge said. "We don't need to worry about that."

"I was just thinking," Reiben said, "that maybe we're lucky to be here—not in the Pacific. I've heard bad stories about the Japanese."

Explosions in the distance reminded them that the war would still be there after their break.

"What are we doing here?" Reiben wondered. "We could be in Caen. It's only ten kilometers away, and it's famous for making women's clothes. And I heard they have pretty girls there."

"Reiben," Miller said, "in case you haven't heard, there's a war going on. They're probably not making anything there now."

The rest of the squad was thinking about this when Miller noticed a runner who was coming their way. The captain nodded to Caparzo, who climbed out of the hole.

"If things hadn't been so terrible on the beach, we'd probably be in Caen right now," Reiben said. "I mean, whose plan was this? Sending 1,000 newly trained guys to fight an important battle."

"You're Rangers," Miller said without expression. "You're specially trained soldiers."

"Back in the US and across the Channel," Mellish said, "they told us what the war was supposed to be like. We talked about it, and we trained—practice battles and everything. But as soon as I jumped off that landing boat I knew. Nothing could have prepared me for this!"

There was an explosion in the distance. The men thought about it—and Mellish's words.

Finally Wade said, "They can't prepare you for it. Maybe they think that if you're surprised enough, the fear won't be so bad."

"Maybe," Mellish said. "But if that was the plan, it didn't work."

Miller asked, "Reiben, tell me—if you had to hit Omaha Beach again, how do you think you'd react the second time?"

Reiben didn't hesitate. "I'd shoot myself before I even got off the boat."

Caparzo jumped into the hole. "Captain," he said, "the Commanding Officer wants to see you at field headquarters immediately."

"Maybe the war's over," Miller said, and climbed out of the hole.

"When you get back, tell us who won," Sarge said.

Miller walked through the men and jeeps and around the shell holes to the badly damaged bunker that the Americans were using as their field headquarters. Inside there were officers, assistants, runners, and radiomen. These men had clean uniforms—not spotted with blood like Miller's.

Lieutenant Colonel Walter Anderson—forty-two, Denver, Colorado—stood up and walked to a large map on the wall. He gestured for Miller to join him.

"The air force was supposed to make an opening for the rest of us," the lieutenant colonel said, shaking his head as he looked at the map. "Instead they dropped men in the wrong places—scattered everywhere. What's your situation, John?"

"Section four is ours now," Miller said.

"Well done. Our casualties?" Anderson asked.

"Thirty-five dead. Twice as many wounded, sir."

Everyone in the room had heard Miller, but no one looked at him. Their silence indicated the horror and respect they all felt.

"It was a difficult assignment. That's why I picked you for it," Anderson told Miller.

"Yes, sir."

"And I have another one for you."

"What is it, sir?"

"It's another difficult one, John." Anderson shook his head. "This one's from the top—General Marshall. Get some coffee and sit down. I've been told to give you all the background."

Half an hour later, when Miller returned to the field, Sergeant Horvath greeted him with a one-word question: "Caen?"

"No. We're taking a squad up to Neuville on a mission."

Sarge frowned. "A captain leading a squad? What kind of mission is that?"

Miller smiled half a smile: "A public-relations mission, Sergeant."

"What?"

"A private in the 101st ... three brothers dead. Our job is to find their little brother and send him home."

"Really? Why Neuville?"

"That's where the Commanding Officer thinks he landed. He's one of those paratroopers who were dropped in the wrong place."

"It isn't going to be easy," Sarge said, "trying to find one soldier in the middle of this big war." He nodded toward the hole where the men were resting. "What about our company?"

"I can pick the best men. The rest will go to Baker Company."

Sarge's eyes opened wide. "They're separating your company for this?"

"First, it's not my company; it's the Army's. Second, there aren't many of us left. Anyway, I want Reiben, Jackson, Wade, of course, Caparzo, Beasley . . ."

"Beasley's dead."

"OK, that kid Mellish. Do we have anybody that speaks French?"

"Not any more. Our translators were killed."

"I'll see if I can find someone," Miller said. "Get the rest of the men together and meet me at the jeeps on the beach."

"Yes, sir."

Miller walked through the men and machines to the tent where the officers had their headquarters. Three corporals were sitting at tables looking at maps.

"I'm looking for Corporal Upham," Miller announced.

One of the boys glanced up from his map and looked at Miller. He had a youthful face and wore thick glasses. He jumped at the sound of a distant explosion.

"Sir," he said, "I'm Upham."

"I understand you speak French and German."

"Yes, sir," said Corporal Tim Upham—twenty-four, Boston, Massachusetts.

Miller came closer. "How's your accent?"

Upham adjusted his glasses. "My French has a slight accent. My German doesn't."

"Good. I'm Captain Miller. You've been reassigned to me. Get your equipment."

"Sir?"

"We're going to Neuville."

Upham smiled nervously and gestured back to his map on the table. "Sir, there are Germans at Neuville."

"That's what I've heard."

"Quite a lot of them, I've heard."

Miller stared at the kid. "Wouldn't you expect to find Germans behind enemy lines, Corporal?"

Upham pointed to himself with both hands. "Sir, I've never been in battle. I'm afraid I won't be any help and I'll just make it harder for you, sir. I'm a mapmaker. I translate."

"I need a translator."

"You do?"

"Both of mine were killed."

Upham became pale. "Sir, I haven't fired a rifle since training."

"Once you learn, you never forget. Where's your equipment?"

"I'll . . . I'll get it, sir. Can I bring my typewriter?"

"Your typewriter?"

"I'm writing a book, and I . . ."

Miller just looked at him.

Upham smiled nervously again. "Well, then . . . a pencil?"

"A little one," Miller answered.

Upham nodded and turned to get his equipment.

"Look at it this way, son," Miller told the boy. "If you live through this, you'll have some good stories to tell."

Chapter 7   On the Road

The dead and wounded had been removed from the beach, and it was now full of activity. Lines of vehicles moved up the sand and off the beach. Among them was a jeep full of soldiers: Captain Miller and his squad of seven men—Sergeant Horvath driving, Corporal Upham, the medic Wade, and Privates Reiben, Caparzo, Jackson, and Mellish.

Soon they were moving fast down a dirt road. The landscape was full of damaged vehicles, abandoned equipment, bodies, and dead animals. Sitting in the front, Upham was pale and his eyes were wide as he looked at the scenery. Miller ignored it and looked at a map.

"Captain, is a question OK?" Reiben asked.

"Maybe."

"Where are you planning to put Private Ryan, sir? There aren't any empty seats in this jeep."

Miller looked at the map and didn't reply.

"I was just wondering," Reiben continued, "if you expect to have more room on the way back."

Miller gestured to the left turn in the road ahead.

Sarge followed the captain's directions. "Are we in radio contact with anybody up there?" he asked.

"Our radios are lost or broken," Miller said. "We're not in contact with anybody."

"What a mission!"

Upham made a quiet noise and spoke. "So, you're all Rangers?" No one responded. "I'm Upham," the corporal said cheerfully, glancing back and offering a hand that nobody shook. Nobody said anything. "I mean ...," Upham said, smiling nervously.

"There's only one reason you're with us," Mellish interrupted.

"Yes. To translate."

"That's right," Miller added. "Upham speaks French and his German is excellent."

The men looked away, and Upham was quiet. After a while Caparzo leaned forward.

"Captain, where's this Ryan from?"

"Iowa, Private Caparzo."

"Iowa?" Reiben repeated. "We're risking our lives to save a farmer?"

Miller thought for a moment and then said, "I'm going to tell you something you're not supposed to know."

The men became quiet and looked at him. The thunder of explosions continued—not as distant.

"I had a look at Ryan's service record," Miller said, "which is excellent."

"That's good," Reiben said.

"But," Miller continued, "it also contained school reports. His grades were excellent and he won the school's Good Citizenship Prize . . . twice. Now—isn't that worth risking your lives for?"

"The perfect American boy," Reiben said. "That's who we're rescuing."

"Yes."

The jeep went around a corner, and Sarge stopped suddenly behind a long line of American vehicles—tanks, trucks, and jeeps. None were moving.

Miller saw a Military Policeman directing traffic on the side of the road. "Lieutenant!" he called.

The policeman saw the captain's stripes on Miller's helmet, came quickly over, and leaned against the jeep.

"We can't let you go ahead," he told Miller. "Artillery shelling is stopping the traffic."

"How's the road to Neuville?" Miller asked him.

"Driving on that road will put your lives in great danger."

Miller and Sarge glanced at each other, knowing they had no choice. They couldn't ignore orders from General Marshall.

"Let us through, lieutenant," Miller said.

"Sir . . ."

"Let us through."

"Yes, sir."

The policeman waved them through. Sarge drove on the side of the road, passing the other vehicles. Soon they were the only vehicle on the road—except damaged jeeps and trucks. Sarge drove on, avoiding the wrecks and the shell holes in the road. Then the jeep went around a destroyed American truck. Miller's eyes searched the landscape to find the source of the artillery shell that had hit it.

They came to a long, straight section of road. Several burning vehicles on it indicated the danger of driving there. Sarge continued down the road while all eyes—except Upham's—nervously searched the surrounding hills.

"Captain," Mellish said, "we're the front leading the Americans now, aren't we?"

"Yes. Everybody else is behind us."

Mellish went on, "You mean the other 150,000 American soldiers with 4,000 vehicles. Right, sir?"

"That's correct."

Suddenly the familiar sound of an artillery shell came toward them and hit the road right in back of them. Sarge drove as fast as he could. Then another shell hit the road in front of them, and the ground shook. Sarge drove on, missing the huge new hole, and asked the captain, "Do you see him?"

Miller saw the artillery gun in the distance. He also saw trees on another hill that would be good cover and were out of the gun's reach.

"Yes," he answered. "This road's one big target!" He pointed toward an empty field between the road and the trees. "Make a new road!"

Sarge turned the jeep off the road and into the empty field. The bombing continued, and Sarge turned the wheel to the right and to the left to avoid the shells. Suddenly they hit a water ditch along the side of the road, and all except Sarge were thrown out of the jeep. Sarge tried to drive out, but the jeep wouldn't move. The other men pushed, but they couldn't move it. The bombing continued.

"Captain," Sarge said anxiously. "They're hitting on both sides of us."

"I know about that," Upham said. "I've read a lot about that method of attack."

The others ignored the corporal and continued trying to move the jeep.

"Listen to me!" Upham said. "The next shell is going to hit us!"

Miller and the men kept pushing, but the men were concerned. They looked toward the sky and waited for the sound of the next shell.

"Captain . . ." Sarge began.

"Push!" Miller commanded. His men pushed. The jeep was almost out of the ditch when they heard the screaming sound of the next shell.

"God," Upham said, almost crying. "It's going to hit us!"

Grabbing his rifle, the captain shouted, "Go! Go! Go!"

The men grabbed everything they could from the jeep—weapons, equipment, anything—and ran.

"Get down!" Miller shouted. And they did—just as the shell hit the jeep and threw it into the air. The men felt the earth shake. Then they heard the sound of mortars.

"Here come the mortars!" Miller shouted. The eight men were already running across the field to the trees as small explosions went off around them. Upham fell. Miller picked him up and dragged him to the trees.

Soon the mortars stopped. Miller's men were lying on the ground and leaning against trees.

"Call out if you're hit," Sarge said.

Nobody spoke. The men stood up slowly and looked around at each other.

"Nobody was hit," Miller said. "Good."

"That's amazing," Wade agreed softly, holding his medic's pack tightly.

Jackson said a prayer.

"Maybe this Private Ryan's good luck," Wade said.

Reiben looked back across the field at the burning jeep. "Let's not be too grateful to that farmer," he smiled, shaking his head. "Now we have to walk the rest of the way, don't we?"

"That's right," Miller said. "Form a line and follow me."

He led his men through the trees to another field and then

through the field to two rows of hedges with a path between them. With the hedges sheltering them, the captain and his men walked on. They began quiet conversations.

"So, where are you from?" Upham asked Mellish. Mellish didn't answer. Upham turned to Caparzo, "How about you? Where are you from?"

"Don't talk to me."

From behind him a more friendly voice—Wade's—said, "I understand you're a writer. What's your book about, Corporal?"

"I don't know—now," Upham answered. "It *was* going to be about how fighting a war together makes men feel like brothers."

Caparzo whispered to Upham, "Why don't you ask the captain where he's from?"

"Why?"

The men around Upham laughed. "It's a private joke," Mellish told him.

Upham was angry. "I'm part of this squad, too!"

No one responded. They walked quietly for a while. Then Reiben went to the front of the line and walked beside Miller. "You know, Captain," he said, "this expedition doesn't make any sense. Maybe you could explain it to me."

"What do you want to know?"

"Well, sir, I'm thinking about the mathematics. What's the sense in risking eight lives to save one? And the guy's not important; he's only a private, sir."

"And we all know how worthless privates are."

"How about an answer, Captain?"

Miller glanced back at the others, saying, "Does anybody want to answer that?"

"Well, Reiben," Wade said immediately, "think of the poor boy's mother."

"Nice, Wade," Miller said, pleased, as if responding to an excellent student. "Very good."

"Well," Reiben responded, "what about *my* mother? What about your mother? We all have mothers. Captain, you have a mother, too."

"We've got orders. And these orders have priority over everything . . . including your mothers."

Chapter 8   Neuville-au-Plain

To the north, the surrounding hills were filled with the sounds of artillery, guns, and mortar and grenade explosions. The village of Neuville-au-Plain was in ruins. One- and two-story houses and buildings, centuries old, were completely destroyed; parts of other structures were left standing. The streets were covered with pieces of wood and stone.

Captain Miller led his squad toward the sound of fighting, which seemed to be just around the corner of a partly destroyed wall. Stopping there, Miller gestured to his men to stay against the wall.

He put his head out and saw a few villagers run across the street. He pulled it back just as a bullet hit the brick near it, but he had seen the American paratroopers—probably from the 101st Airborne—who sat in doorways along the alley, shooting at the unseen enemy.

"Thunder!" Miller called, giving the code word that American soldiers used to identify themselves.

"Flash!" came the code response. "Come across!"

Miller looked at his men. "When I call for you, run across—one at a time."

Then he ran left and right across the street, avoiding the German bullets. He took cover in a doorway across the way.

Upham was pale as he watched his captain.

Jackson, seeing this, said, "Don't worry, kid. They can't kill the captain."

"Jackson's right," Reiben added. "It's like magic. We've all seen him avoid German bullets. They can't hit him."

"That's right," Caparzo agreed, grinning.

"Nobody's safe from bullets," Sarge said. "*Nobody!*"

Across the street, Miller ran out of the doorway and down the alley to a group of ten dirty, exhausted paratroopers sitting against a wall.

"Wade! Wounded!" Miller called back down the alley.

"We're glad to see you!" said Goldman—twenty-three, Chicago, Illinois. "Sarge, our assistance has arrived!" he called to his sergeant.

Sergeant William Hill—twenty-nine, Pensicola, Florida—hurried down the line of men to Miller. "How many of you are there?"

Wade arrived, and Miller sent him to take care of the wounded paratroopers.

"I'm sorry to disappoint you," he told Hill. "We're not your assistance. There are only eight of us."

"What are you doing here, sir?" asked Hill.

"We're on a special assignment. We're looking for Private James Ryan."

"Why?" the sergeant asked, confused and annoyed.

Reiben arrived. Miller nodded to him and then asked Sergeant Hill, "Is he here?"

"He might be in a mixed group on the other side of town. It's hard to get there ... the Germans have divided us. What's his name?"

"Ryan," Miller said. "James. Private. He dropped with you guys—the 101st—when you parachuted down."

The rest of Miller's men arrived one by one, successfully avoiding the bullets. Then Hill called, "Send the runner here now!"

Private Harold Nelson—twenty-one, Omaha, Nebraska— hurried to Hill.

"Find Captain Hamill," the sergeant told him. "There's a squad here looking for someone named Private James Ryan. He was probably dropped in the wrong place with the 101st."

The kid nodded, looked over the wall, then ran around the corner and down the streets. The gunfire began again. Miller leaned out and watched as a bullet hit Nelson's leg and he fell to one knee. While he tried to crawl to cover, he was hit again and killed.

Quietly, Sergeant Hill said, "They know our two sections aren't in contact. They're going to kill runners, because they're our link."

Miller, joined by Sergeant Hill, walked to the end of the alley and looked out. "There are some two-story buildings on the next street," Hill said. "There's good cover on the left."

"OK. We'll go there."

The men gathered around Miller, and he instructed them. Upham was shaking. Miller's hand was shaking, too, but no one noticed—except Miller. The captain led them up the street to the higher buildings. They ran quickly, stopping in doorways for cover and searching the windows and rooftops for snipers.

Reiben and Upham stopped in a doorway together. "So, where's the captain from, anyway?" Upham whispered.

Reiben whispered back, "If you find out, you win."

Jackson stopped in a nearby doorway and heard this whispered discussion. "It's over three hundred dollars now."

Mellish moved quickly past, informing Upham: "The company has a bet. Give us five dollars and you can join in."

Moments later the entire group was moving along a stone wall.

"Doesn't anyone know where he's from or what he did?" Upham asked the squad members.

Sarge grabbed Upham and dragged him along. "I've been with him for a long time—since Kasserine Pass," Horvath said, "and I don't have any idea."

From ahead Caparzo said, "I know about the captain. I looked inside his pack once."

"You don't know anything," Jackson shouted.

"You can say that if you want to," Caparzo said. "I'm just waiting for the bet money to increase. Then I'll tell you, and the money will be mine."

"Shhhh!" Sarge said from up ahead.

Then they were quiet as the squad came closer to their destination. Soon they stood beside a house that was missing an outside wall; nothing else was damaged, and they could see into the rooms on the floor above them. A noise came from one of them, and they prepared to shoot.

Hill called out the code word: "Thunder!"

There was no response. He called again, and a voice responded in French.

"Don't shoot!" Upham called. "They're civilians!"

A man, obviously a local resident, stepped into view on the second floor with his hands raised. A woman with an infant in her arms followed him.

"Ask them where the Germans are," Miller instructed Upham.

Upham spoke with them in French.

"What's he saying?" Miller asked.

"I don't know exactly," Upham said. "He's talking very quickly . . . something about taking the children . . ."

The couple stepped out of view for a few moments, and then returned with a girl, about four years old, and a boy, a little older. The father picked up the crying girl and held her by her wrists in the air, lowering her toward the soldiers.

"They want us to take their children," Upham said quietly.

"Tell them we can't take children," Miller said.

"Don't cry," Caparzo said to the little girl, smiling at her and making funny faces. He reached up for her. Her father stopped holding her, and she jumped down with delight into Caparzo's arms.

Seeing this, the father pulled the boy away from his mother and lowered him, too. Mellish and Jackson reached up and received the boy, lifting him gently down.

Miller tried not to be angry.

Upham said to him, "They think the children will be safe with us."

"It's not safe with us," Miller said angrily. Then he added more kindly, "Tell them it's not safe anywhere, but it's especially not safe with us. Tell them."

Upham nodded and spoke in French.

Caparzo played with the little girl. "She reminds me of my niece," he said.

"Caparzo!" Miller said. "Put that child down!"

But the child was having fun, and Caparzo was happy holding her.

"Captain, let's do the decent thing," he said softly. "Let's take these kids down the road to the next town."

Miller was affected by Caparzo's desire. But he said firmly, "We're not here to do the decent thing. We're here to follow orders. *You're* here to follow orders."

"Captain . . ."

"Now hand that kid back to her parents."

Miller's men were surprised. They knew he was a decent man and didn't understand why he was being so heartless.

Caparzo looked at the girl in his arms, and she laughed. His eyes were wet.

"Give her back to her parents, Caparzo," Miller said gently. "Do it. Now."

"But, sir," Caparzo said. "I don't think—"

41

Just then a sniper's bullet hit the private in the chest. He dropped the little girl and fell. She landed on her feet—not injured, but confused and frightened.

Everyone screamed, but Caparzo's screams could be heard above them all. "I'm shot! I'm shot!"

Miller and most of his squad ran across the street and hid behind a pile of stones and bricks. But Wade and Upham stayed in the killing zone. Wade went to his wounded friend, and Upham went to the two children. They were still standing in the same place—motionless.

"I'm shot!" Caparzo screamed, bleeding. "Oh, God, I'm shot!"

"You're going to be fine," Wade said a moment before Sarge ran out, grabbed the medic, and pulled him to cover. Miller ran out, too. He grabbed Upham by the collar and pulled him away from the frightened children.

Another bullet went by them and hit a stone wall. The children, still not moving but now crying, were unharmed. They weren't targets, Miller knew, but while they were near the soldiers, they were in danger.

Wade moved next to his captain. "We have to get Caparzo out of there."

"Stay here, Wade," Miller said. "That's an order."

Suddenly Caparzo stopped screaming. He reached into his shirt pocket and took out an envelope. Then he tried to sit up, but he couldn't. "Oh, God . . . oh . . . oh, God."

Miller couldn't show his men how bad he felt. Suddenly there was an explosion nearby. He ran out, grabbed the children in his arms, and dragged them to cover. He put them in a doorway, motioning for them to stay low.

Across the street in the house with the missing wall, the parents were standing close together, the mother still holding her infant in her arms. They were crying with relief—their children were in their sight and safe.

"Where's the sniper?" Miller asked Jackson.

Jackson pointed down the street to a small house on the green hillside about a third of a kilometer beyond the village. "That's where I'd be." He reached into his pack and took out a special attachment that would help him see the distant sniper clearly.

Caparzo was losing energy. He held up his bloody letter, offering it to anyone who would take it. "Help me . . . somebody . . . I'm losing my blood . . . help . . ."

Jackson put the attachment on his sniper's rifle.

"Help me," Caparzo cried softly, still holding out his letter. ". . . This letter . . . important . . . it's to my father . . . but it's all bloody . . ."

"Don't talk," Wade said. Then he said to Miller, "You have to let me go over there."

"Stay here, Wade."

Caparzo held up his letter toward his friends—to Wade and Mellish. "Don't want Papa, Mama . . . to see the blood . . . Copy it . . ."

Jackson prayed and then fired. The German sniper in the distant house dropped his rifle and fell to the floor—dead. Jackson lowered his rifle, nodded to Miller and the rest, and prayed again.

"Go!" Miller said to Wade.

Wade and Mellish ran to Caparzo, but he was already dead. Miller approached, and Wade stared at him angrily. The captain walked through the dead private's blood to his body and bent down, taking one of Caparzo's dog tags and putting it in his pocket. Then he stood and nodded in the direction they were going.

Chapter 9   Private Ryan

"Jackson," Miller said. "Take Mellish. Check the sniper's house. We don't want any more danger coming from there."

"Yes, sir," Jackson said, and Mellish joined him. They walked past Reiben and Wade, who was bandaging a deep wound in Reiben's forehead.

"Forget Private Ryan," Reiben said angrily. "Forget him."

"Stop it," Jackson said as he passed the two men.

"Caparzo's just the first of us to die trying to save Private Ryan," Reiben complained. "You'll see."

"Private Ryan didn't kill Caparzo," Wade responded. "A German sniper did."

While his men continued their journey down the street to the town center, Miller looked at Caparzo's bloody letter. He started to pick it up and realized that Wade was also looking at it. The two men hesitated, staring at each other. Then Wade picked up the letter, put it in his pocket, and joined the rest of the men going down the street.

Miller glanced up at the man and his wife. Their expressions told him that they finally understood. The Americans were not going to take their two children to a safer place. He smiled and waved goodbye to the children in the doorway behind him. Then he followed his men, carefully surveying the street and the surrounding buildings. He did not want to lose another man ...

Jackson and Mellish entered the small house on the hillside, and Mellish stayed downstairs while Jackson went up. He looked around the small rooms carefully. They were empty. The last room he entered had a huge hole in the floor. Looking down through the hole, he saw the body of the sniper he had shot.

Mellish stood near the dead body, looking up. "Come down, Jackson," he said. "Let's get out of here."

Soon the two men joined Miller and the squad, and Sergeant

Hill and his men, in the town center. The sound of bullets made the men a little nervous, and they kept their guns and rifles ready as they walked.

Miller and Hill stopped in a doorway together. Miller pointed to a machine gun in a third-floor window across the open area, indicating that they needed to move quickly.

Suddenly a voice from that window called out: "Thunder!" A very American voice.

Hill called back, "Flash!"

The captain and sergeant smiled and then stepped out and led their men across the open area. When they reached the building, they separated and went in different doors.

Miller's group entered a large room full of broken furniture, wood from the ceiling, and broken bricks. As they walked through the room, the captain saw five men sitting in the shadows against the wall. He didn't look closely at these men; he'd been told that this building was controlled by the Americans. Then the men in the shadows turned around and faced them. Miller realized that their uniforms were gray—not green. They were Germans!

The Germans and Americans, equally shocked, looked at each other and then began to shout in their native languages for the others to surrender. After a few minutes they stopped, and it was quiet—no one spoke or moved.

Suddenly one of the young Germans got scared and raised his gun. Before Miller could react, machine-gun fire rained down and the five Germans were dead.

When it was quiet again, Sergeant Hill and his men entered the room, ready to shoot. The captain above called down to them. Miller and his men stood up and moved so they could see who had saved their lives. Upstairs, they saw a dozen American paratroopers staring down at them. Their leader, Captain DeWayne Hamill—thirty-one, San Diego, California—looked confused.

"We've come for Private Ryan," Miller explained.

Hamill and his paratroopers came downstairs and joined Miller's squad and Hill's men. Together they left the building and went to the northern edge of the city. This section of the city of Neuville was controlled by Americans. The sight of American tanks around its edge made Miller feel safe.

When they came to train tracks, Miller and his men paused while Hamill spoke to the lieutenant standing there. "Bring Private Ryan here," he ordered.

"Ryan!" the lieutenant called out to the paratroopers standing along the edge of the section. "Come here!"

A helmeted soldier came out of a hole and ran to them.

"Sir," the man said. "Private James Ryan reporting as ordered, sir."

"This is Captain Miller," Hamill told him. "He wants to talk to you."

"Private," Miller said gently, "I'm afraid I have some bad news for you."

"Sir?"

"There's no easy way to say this, son," Miller said. He paused briefly and then continued, "Your brothers are dead."

"What?" The boy's face became pale and he dropped to the ground. "Dead . . . dead, sir? All of them are dead?"

Miller nodded seriously down at him. "We've been sent to take you home, son. You're going home."

"Oh, my God," the boy said, and he began to cry. "My brothers . . . oh, my God, my sweet little brothers . . ."

Hamill patted the boy's shoulder. "We're sorry for your loss, James. I can't tell you how much."

"How . . . how did they . . . die?" Ryan asked.

"They were killed in action," Miller said.

The boy frowned, confused, "What . . . what kind of action?"

"I don't know the details. I'm truly sorry."

"This *can't* be . . ."

"It's always hard to accept something like this."

The boy's tears stopped. "No, I mean it can't be true. Ned and Richie, they're both in elementary school."

Now Miller was the one who was surprised.

"Is that it?" Ryan asked. "A school-yard accident?"

Miller studied the boy. "You are James Ryan?"

"Yes."

"James F.?"

"That's right. So they *are* dead?" And his tears began again.

Miller tried again, "You're James Francis Ryan?"

He shook his head. "James Frederick Ryan."

Miller wondered if there was a mistake on the middle name. He asked, "Iowa?"

"Minnesota." He was still crying. "Does . . . does this mean my brothers are all right?"

"Yes, I'm sure they are," Miller said. "We're looking for another James Ryan."

James Frederick Ryan was still crying. "Are you sure my brothers are OK? How do you *know* they are?"

"This is just a mistake, son. I'm sorry."

"So you're not taking me home?"

"No. We're not." Ryan sat on a box, crying. Some of his friends came over to comfort him; other paratroopers standing nearby had heard the discussion and were laughing.

Feeling bad, Miller stood close to Captain Hamill and said, "I'm sorry for the mistake."

They walked away from the train tracks. Hamill stayed with them. Sarge moved up to Miller and asked, "So, where is *our* Ryan?"

"I don't know," Miller said. He turned to Hamill. "Are you in contact with your Commanding Officer?"

"No," he answered. But he wanted to help. "What unit is your Ryan in?"

"Baker Company, 506th."

Hamill called to Sergeant Hill, who was smoking with his men. "That guy who broke his foot is from the 506th, isn't he?"

"Yes—Charlie Company, I think."

Hamill looked at Miller. "It's not Baker Company, but it's a start."

"It's more than I know now. Where do we go?"

"Follow me . . ."

Hamill and Miller went to a bombed-out grocery store where the wounded of the 101st were sitting. Hamill spoke to one of the paratroopers.

The boy looked up at the two captains and said, "Ryan? Sorry, I don't know him."

"Where were you dropped?" Miller asked.

"Near Vierville."

"Well, how did you get here?"

"Sir, our plane was fired at, and our pilot tried to avoid the bullets. We turned around a lot, and this is where we landed. I'm just glad to be alive."

Miller nodded. "Did anyone in Baker Company say where they would be dropped?"

"No, sir . . . but I know Baker Company had the same meeting place as us."

Miller was satisfied to finally get some information. He took out a map and unfolded it.

"Good," he said. "Show me."

Soon Miller and Hamill rejoined the squad and Sergeant Hill and his men, who were waiting outside the store.

"Do we have someplace to go?" Sarge asked Miller.

"Yes," Miller said. "We'll wait until dark and then leave." He looked at Hamill and asked, "Do you have a place where we can sleep?"

"Of course," Hamill said. "Sergeant Hill, take them to the church."

"Yes, sir," Hill said. The men followed the sergeant, leaving the two captains alone.

Miller and Hamill sat down and talked about the war. They didn't often find someone they could talk to. After a while, Hamill shook his head and said, "We could use your help here."

"I'd like to help. But orders are orders."

"I know. Anyway, I understand what you're doing. Good luck with your mission, friend."

"Thank you, Captain."

"Find that lucky soldier and send him home."

They talked for another hour, and then Miller went to the church to join his men. Jackson was on guard outside the building.

"Thunder," Miller said.

"Flash," Jackson responded.

"Jackson," Miller said. "Why are you the only one in the squad who doesn't think I'm heartless."

"I *do* think you're heartless," he said. "That's your job right now, and I thank God you're doing it. And you do it well, sir."

Miller smiled at Jackson, nodded, went inside, and walked through the ruins of the building. Wade was on one of the benches, writing something. Without looking, Miller knew what Wade was doing: copying Caparzo's letter from the bloody paper to a clean one.

"We'll leave in two hours," he announced. "Try to get some sleep."

Wade glanced at Miller angrily and continued copying. Miller walked to another part of the room and noticed that Upham was lying on a bench, shaking. The captain paused and quietly asked, "How are you doing, Corporal?"

Upham smiled weakly. "This is good for me, sir. All of it."

"How, son?"

49

Upham sat up. "War is an education. I can use what I'm learning in my writing."

He paused; his shaking had stopped. "Captain ... where are you from?"

"Why?"

"I was just wondering ... what you did in civilian life?"

"How much money has been bet now?" Miller asked.

Upham grinned. "It's over three hundred dollars."

Miller thought about that. "When it's five hundred, I'll tell you, and we'll share the money."

"If that's how you feel, why don't we wait until it's a thousand dollars?"

Miller shook his head. "I might not live that long."

Upham stopped grinning as he realized that his captain wasn't joking. "OK. Five hundred."

Miller went to the side of the church, sat on the floor, and opened his maps. He studied them, using a small light. The men around him were sleeping. The hand holding the light began to shake.

"How long has it been shaking?"

The voice was Sarge's. Horvath sat next to his captain, who answered, "It started a long time ago—back in Portsmouth when we got on the boats. It doesn't always do this."

"Maybe you should think about getting a different job."

Miller laughed gently. "Yes. This one isn't much fun."

The two men talked about other battles they had been in together. Miller shook his head and explained softly, "Every time one of your boys gets killed, you tell yourself that you saved the lives of two, three, ten, maybe a hundred other men and boys."

"That's a good way to think about it."

"Do you know how many men have been killed under my command?"

"No."

"Caparzo made ninety-four. That means I probably saved the lives of ten times that many. Maybe twenty times. If you do the math, you can choose the mission over the men—every time."

"But this time," Sarge said, "the mission *is* a man."

"If that kid today had been our Private Ryan, would he have been worth Caparzo?" Miller asked.

"His mother might think so."

"I have a mother; you have a mother; Caparzo had a mother . . . I hope this Private James Francis Ryan is very special. I hope he does something great with his life—like cure cancer. Because the truth is, I wouldn't trade ten Ryans for one Caparzo."

Horvath thought for a minute and then said, "You know, Ryan doesn't just have a mother . . . he has a captain, too, who probably feels the same about him as you do about these kids."

Miller's hand was shaking. He stared at it, trying to make it stop. Then he stood up and looked at his watch.

"It's time to get up," he called to his men. "Let's go!"

And the men woke up, put on their equipment, and followed their captain out of the shelter of the church—out into the night and the waiting war.

Chapter 10   New Hope

Miller and his men walked cautiously along the edge of a field. The only light came from the moon, and the only sounds were the sounds of night birds and insects.

Miller was proud of his boys—his men. At Omaha Beach they had been new to fighting, but now they were experienced soldiers. He noticed that Jackson and Wade were walking too close to each other, and he gestured to them to move apart.

Suddenly there was a flash in the sky. Soon the entire sky was lighted with exploding shells. The soldiers stopped, and their eyes turned upward to watch the show.

Miller knew that this battle wouldn't reach them. He quietly got the men's attention, and they began walking again. They walked all night through fields and farmland.

As the morning light began to appear, Reiben, who had been unusually quiet for a while, asked a question: "What's the best thing that could happen. Do you know?"

Miller laughed, wanting his men to be cheerful. "OK. What's the best thing that could happen?"

"The best thing," Reiben said, "would be that we find Ryan— dead."

"And why's that best?"

"Sir, consider the possibilities. A: Ryan is alive, and we have to take him back to the beach. You won't let him help carry our equipment like he should. We have to take care of him so he can be sent home to his mother. We all get killed trying to keep him alive."

"OK," Miller said. He sounded like he agreed with Reiben, which made the men smile.

Reiben continued: "Or B: Ryan's dead. And you, sir, make us check the body carefully to be sure that he's dead and that he's the right Private Ryan. Then the Germans kill us while we're checking."

"I don't like that possibility," Miller said.

"Neither do I, sir," said Reiben. "So let's consider possibility C: we find Ryan and he's wounded."

"That's not good," Mellish said.

"That's the worst possibility," Reiben agreed. "If that happens, he won't be able to help carry our equipment and *we'll* have to carry *his* equipment. *And* we'll have to carry Private Ryan, too."

"That could happen," Miller said.

"That's what I'm saying, sir. The best situation is D: he's dead and has been dead for a long time. We take his dog tags and hurry back to the beach."

"Do we take his body?" Mellish asked.

"No! We leave him for a burial squad."

"I have a better idea," Mellish said. "We shoot Reiben and leave his body here. Then we change his dog tags so they say 'RYAN' and send them to Ryan's mother."

"That's an interesting idea," Miller said without laughing. "It's a possibility."

"I'm sorry, sir," Reiben said, "but I like my idea better."

Walking through the night, they didn't see any other people. Then about an hour after sunrise they heard sounds of activity on the other side of a hedge. Looking through the hedge, the squad saw hundreds of American soldiers—mostly paratroopers—and French civilians. There were six American planes in the field; one was damaged. Three sides of the field were lined with hedges; the fourth was a dirt road.

As Miller's squad walked onto the field, a group from the 506th was taking several German prisoners to a special area. Miller knew that his boys were seeing the enemy for the first time. He knew they would be shocked. The Germans looked so normal—like themselves—and so young.

Standing by the damaged plane, where the wounded were gathering, a young American pilot motioned to them, and they walked over. Wade went to take care of the wounded, and Miller stopped in front of the pilot. "Tell me what happened, Lieutenant."

William Dewindt—twenty-five, Scottsdale, Arizona—replied, "We were hit. Twenty-two men were killed."

"Where's the company? Who are all these people?"

"The guys we brought here left during the first night. Others keep coming. Sooner or later an officer will come and make a company from this mixed group. You're a small group. You must have had heavy casualties, too, sir."

"No," Miller said, "we're on a special assignment, Lieutenant. We're looking for Private James Ryan, Baker Company, of the 506th. Have you seen him?"

"I don't know if I've seen him, sir," Dewindt responded. "A lot of guys have come and gone."

Miller glanced over at his medic and asked, "Did you find anything?"

Wade looked up and said, "He's not among these men."

"Upham," Miller said. "Talk to all of these paratroopers. Look for Ryan or news about him."

"Yes, sir." And Upham left.

Dewindt shook a small bag, tied on his belt. "You might want to look at these, too."

Miller didn't understand. "What are they?"

The pilot untied the bag and handed it to the captain. "That's my dog-tag collection," he said. "There are more of them than I can count. One could be your man's."

Miller took the bag and handed it to Jackson, saying, "See if you can find Private Ryan's."

"Yes, sir."

"I'll help," Reiben offered.

They sat on the grass, and Mellish joined them. They passed the bag, each taking a handful, checking them, and then putting them on the empty bag. When they finished, they refilled the bag, and Jackson handed it back to Dewindt. "Ryan's isn't here, sir," he reported.

Miller nodded to Dewindt and walked toward Upham, who was in the middle of the field. The squad followed.

"Ryan's not here," Upham reported.

"Now what will we do, sir?" Sarge asked Miller.

Miller stared at him and walked toward the road, where more civilians and wounded were coming to join the soldiers. "The radios don't work. No one's in command . . ."

His men followed him, feeling concerned. "Is he complaining," Reiben whispered to Mellish, "or going crazy?"

Miller stopped suddenly, and everybody else did, too. "I have an idea," he said. "Let's separate into two groups and wander around the countryside calling Ryan's name. Sooner or later, he'll hear us."

"Good idea, sir," Sarge said. Was Miller joking or not? "But that could take a lot of time."

"OK, let's ask the local civilians," Miller said. "Maybe they've seen him."

An old couple walking down the road into the field halted as the captain moved quickly toward them, asking if they knew Ryan. The old couple spoke in French and moved quickly away.

Upham whispered to Reiben and Mellish, "*They* think he's crazy."

A group of paratroopers walked by them, taking more German prisoners to the special area. Miller called to them, "One hundred first! Do any of you know a guy named Ryan?"

The paratroopers shook their heads, no. But as the line of men passed by, Miller kept asking, becoming increasingly frustrated. His men were worried.

Then a voice from down the line called out to another paratrooper, "Joe, isn't Michaelson's friend's name Ryan? The one from Company C?"

"I think so, yes!" a voice called back.

"Bring Michaelson here!" the paratrooper shouted.

Soon two paratroopers stood before Miller and his squad.

"Do either of you know a guy named Ryan?" Miller asked.

"Michaelson knows a guy named Ryan, Captain," the paratrooper on the left said. "But you'll have to speak loudly. A grenade went off next to him and damaged his hearing."

"Do you know Ryan?" Miller shouted to Michaelson.

"Who?"

"Ryan! Do you know Ryan?"

"Jimmy Ryan?"

Behind him, Miller's men listened closely now. Reiben whispered to Mellish, "He's not crazy—he's magic."

Miller was grinning and nodding. "James Francis Ryan?"

"Jimmy Ryan? What?"

Miller turned to his men. "Who's got a pencil?"

"Sir . . ." It was Upham, holding out a short pencil. ". . . I have only this small one, sir."

The captain and corporal looked at each other without expression, but their eyes shared a smile as they remembered their last conversation about the pencil.

Then Miller asked, "Do you have paper, Upham?"

"Yes, sir," he said and held up a small notebook.

"Good. Now write this down: 'Do you know James Francis Ryan?'"

Upham nodded, wrote the message, and held up the notebook for Michaelson to read.

"Of course I know him!" Michaelson shouted. "He's my best friend."

"Does he know where Ryan is?" Miller said to Upham, who wrote the message and held it up.

Michaelson nodded and said, "Yes. We missed our drop zone by about thirty kilometers. Jimmy, me, and a couple other guys were coming here to our meeting point! We met a colonel who was gathering men to go to Ramelle . . . That's the last time I saw him."

The men of Miller's squad smiled at each other, excited by this news; their expedition had turned into a real mission.

Miller patted Michaelson's shoulder. "Thank you!"

"What?"

The captain sighed and told the other paratrooper, "Thank him for me, please, when he can hear again."

A minute later Miller had opened a map on the grass, and his men gathered around him. He pointed as he said, "We're here— Ramelle is there. On the Merderet River, about twenty-five kilometers away."

Sarge thought for a second. "Why Ramelle?" he asked.

Miller unfolded the map more and pointed as he spoke. He didn't notice that his hand was shaking, but his men did—they were staring at his trembling fingers, not at the map.

"The target has always been Cherbourg," Miller said. "We can't go on to Paris unless we take an important port. The Germans know that, of course, and they'll cross the Merderet and hit us when we turn to go to Cherbourg. That makes any village on the river with a bridge very important."

And the captain pointed at the map—right at Ramelle, where the bridge was clearly indicated.

"That's where we'll find Private Ryan," he said.

He looked at his men and realized that they were staring at his trembling hand. Without speaking, he folded up the map. Then he said, "Let's go!"

Chapter 11   Germans

Morning had ended and afternoon begun as the soldiers walked through the French countryside.

"I think fighting in the Pacific is easier," Reiben said to the others."

"I don't know," Mellish said.

"The Germans look like us, but the Japanese don't. Shooting Japanese is easier."

Miller, at the front of the line, smiled to himself as he realized that the German prisoners had affected his boys.

"I don't have any trouble shooting Germans," Mellish said.

"Killing a man is killing a man," Wade said. "It doesn't matter what he looks like."

"There's never been a German worth anything," Reiben observed. "They're all stupid and always have been. It's in their blood."

Miller glanced back at him. "What about Beethoven, the great musician? Do you remember him?"

"He's stupid," Reiben said.

"What about Immanuel Kant, the great philosopher?" Upham asked.

"He's stupid, too," Reiben responded.

They walked on. They could hear the sound of gunfire in the distance.

"They can't all be stupid," Upham said.

"Yes, they can," Reiben said.

Wade said, "Do I understand you correctly, Reiben? You think there isn't a decent man, woman, and child in their entire country."

"That's right."

"Reiben, you're the most uneducated person I've ever met," Wade said.

"Maybe," Reiben said, "but I'm not stupid."

"Let's vote on that," Mellish said.

"OK. OK. Name one decent German. Just one . . ."

Nobody said anything.

Reiben grinned. "It's not easy, is it?"

"Albert Schweitzer," Wade said.

"Who?"

"Albert Schweitzer. He's a German."

"It's not important, but who is he? He already sounds stupid."

Wade shook his head, frustrated. "Albert Schweitzer's the most famous doctor in history! He spent the last thirty years in Africa, helping natives."

"Why did he do that?" Reiben asked.

Wade responded angrily: "Because he was trying to help other people! Because he isn't selfish like you, Reiben! Albert Schweitzer is the reason I became a doctor. The next time you're wounded, you'd better hope I feel like helping you!"

Reiben grinned and shook his head. "I thought you said that both your parents are doctors."

"That's right, Reiben. What about it?"

Miller interrupted the discussion. "Reiben, lose an argument—just once, OK? Albert Schweitzer was not stupid. You, however, are."

"OK, OK," Reiben said. Then he was quiet.

Miller changed places with Sarge and walked beside Wade. Looking back to see that Reiben couldn't hear, he whispered, "Albert Schweitzer was born in Alsace." Wade looked at Miller with surprise. "His family was German," Miller whispered, "but he's officially French. It'll be our secret."

Then Wade smiled at Miller. It was a small smile, but it felt very good to the captain. He was glad to be friends with his medic again.

The field had trees instead of hedges at the end of it. The seven soldiers walked carefully through the trees. When they came to waist-high grass at the edge of the next field, Miller stopped his men and carefully surveyed the landscape. He saw pieces of a German radio tower and bunkers that had been destroyed— probably by the artillery shells that had flashed in the sky last night. The surrounding field was full of bomb holes and dead cows.

Miller motioned his men to stay where they were and to stay low. He moved, keeping low, to the edge of the trees and into the grass. Then he waved at Horvath and Jackson to join him, and Sarge saw something interesting nearby.

"Look at this, Captain," he whispered.

Miller turned and saw nearby trees, smaller ones at the edge of the field, that had a lot of bullet holes in them. "When did that happen?" he asked.

Sarge looked closely. "Recently."

"Do you think it happened after that tower and the bunkers got hit?"

"Yes."

Wade quietly but urgently called to them, and Miller, the sergeant, and the sharpshooter hurried to him, keeping low. Wade was pale as he pointed to a trail of blood—fresh blood—which led to an area in the grass where they could see the bodies of paratroopers. Miller and Sarge rose just enough to see more bodies. It was a small squad—like theirs. The bodies were in pieces.

Miller looked over the top of the grass, studying the slope to the bunkers. "Sarge, do you see that hole below the bunker?"

"Yes," Sarge nodded and sat low next to the captain.

"Look hard—you can see the sand bags."

The rest of the squad gathered around Miller and Sarge. Upham, eyes wide, looked at the bodies and asked, "What do you think did this? A machine gun?"

Jackson nodded. "Yes."

"*One* gun did that?"

Mellish, also looking at the bodies said, "They're paratroopers . . . Maybe one of them's Private Ryan."

"Look at their badges," Miller said. "They're from the 82nd."

"Sir," Reiben said, and he pointed off to the left. "Why don't we go that way and stay in the trees—quickly and quietly. They'll never know we were here."

Miller was putting bullets into his rifle.

"I mean, sir," Reiben continued, "why should we ask for trouble when we can go around it?"

"We're not going around it," Miller said. "We're going to take it."

"Maybe Reiben's right, sir," Jackson said. "I mean, we left Germans behind before . . ."

"We left them for the air force to hit," Miller said. "But the air force isn't going to come after one machine gun, is it? That's what they pay foot soldiers like us to do."

"Sir," Mellish said. "We can complete our mission without doing this . . . I mean, this *isn't* our mission . . ."

"You think we should just leave this machine gun for the next company that comes here. Right?" Miller said, looking at Mellish. "The next company might not see these bodies hidden in the grass."

"That's not what I meant, sir. But it seems like an unnecessary risk, considering our goal."

"Our goal is to win the war, Private."

"I thought we were here to save Ryan."

"That's right," Reiben said. "I mean, it'd be great to kill these Germans, but think of Private Ryan. Think of his mother."

"Reiben . . ." Miller began angrily.

"I just have a bad feeling about this one, sir."

"Really?" Miller asked, taking two grenades from his pack. "And when did you ever have a *good* feeling about anything?"

Reiben didn't have an answer to that.

"OK," Miller said. "Three runners will go out—one at a time. Mellish, you go to the right. I'll go up the middle. Who wants to go to the left?" He hung the grenades on his pack, unaware that his hand was shaking badly.

When no one volunteered, Miller frowned and shouted, "Who's going to go to the left?"

"I will, sir," Jackson said.

"Good. Jackson goes to the left." He looked at Mellish and Jackson and said, "Shoot and run fast until we're close enough to use grenades."

"Maybe I should go up the middle, sir," Sarge said. "We really shouldn't risk our—"

"You can't run fast enough," Miller interrupted.

"I'll go left, then," Sarge said.

"You'll stop talking," Miller shouted. "Sending both of us *would* be a stupid risk. Reiben, you'll be the main shooter." Reiben nodded seriously. "Keep your bullets where you can reach them," Miller continued. "You'll shoot first. When you fire, we'll go." Reiben nodded again; Mellish and Jackson nodded, too. Miller added, "Give the runners extra grenades."

Reiben and Upham handed their grenades to the runners, and the three men got in position and waited. Miller nodded to Reiben, who began firing.

Keeping low, under Reiben's covering fire, Mellish ran toward the hill to the right. Then Miller ran down the center, and Jackson to the left. Each of them jumped into a shell hole for cover before the machine gun knew that they were there.

Then the machine gun started firing heavily. Just before he jumped into his hole, Miller saw the flat-helmeted Germans. There were three of them: one firing, one putting bullets in the machine gun, and one watching the Americans. From the grass, Reiben, Sarge, and Upham fired back.

Mellish called to Miller, "Who are those guys?"

"They're special paratroopers," Miller shouted. "They don't give up."

"I was hoping for young soldiers," Mellish said, holding his rifle tightly.

"If we can make them shoot long enough," Miller said, "they'll use all their bullets. They'll have to stop and put more bullets in. Then we can throw the grenades." He paused and then shouted, "Move out!"

Mellish ran toward the next hole, shooting at the machine gun as he ran. The Germans saw him.

While the Germans were turning their machine gun toward Mellish, Jackson ran to a steel section from the destroyed radio tower. He took cover there as the machine gun turned again and started firing in his direction, hitting the metal.

Miller saw what was happening and ran toward a trench near the bottom of the hill. The machine gun tried to hit him, but its angle was wrong. Instead it swung toward Mellish, who was shooting and running to another hole. Miller jumped into his trench and ran along it. He looked up and saw Jackson running along the steel section, bullets hitting the metal.

Miller smiled a little. The machine gun had been firing continuously, and none of them had been hit. He glanced at Mellish and signaled him to follow. Then he ran out of his trench toward another shell hole, with the private following and the machine gun firing over them.

Both men jumped into the shell hole and were surprised to see that they weren't alone. Two American paratroopers were already there. They were dead.

"Where did they come from?" Mellish asked, moving away from the dead men.

"Something's wrong," Miller said, turning pale. "That machine gun couldn't have hit these boys. It's at the wrong angle."

The machine gun fired bullets toward them, but they didn't reach their target.

Then silence.

Miller waited. He wondered what was happening.

Jackson raced from behind the steel section, shooting toward the machine gun as he ran to a trench. The machine gun fired back, and Jackson fell to the ground.

"Jackson!" Mellish screamed.

Silence again.

"Grenades," Miller ordered.

He and Mellish prepared grenades. Both rose, threw their grenades, and quickly sat down again.

"We threw them too high," Miller said, knowing the grenades had landed on the slope above the machine gun.

More silence.

"Again!" Miller shouted.

He threw another grenade and heard it hit a sand bag. The first two grenades exploded, but did no damage. Mellish threw his next grenade—a perfect throw, but one of the Germans picked up the two grenades and threw them back out. They exploded over the field, but Miller and Mellish weren't wounded.

Someone was screaming: "Oh, God!"

It was Wade's voice, coming from the grass, where he had been moving toward the wounded Jackson.

"Another gun!" The medic stood up and shouted, waving his arms and signaling. His Red Cross armband was visible. "Sir, there's another gun!"

Miller turned and saw, to the left, another flat-helmeted German. He stood up from where he had been hidden by the grass, his hands holding a machine gun.

Suddenly three things happened at almost the same time.

The machine gun in the hole below the bunker began firing at the new target—Wade—and Miller watched the medic fall into the grass.

Jackson, his arm bloody, leaned on his rifle and fired at the second machine gunner in the grass. He hit his helmet, and the sniper fell and died.

And finally, Mellish threw another grenade at the machine gun in the hole. The three Germans tried to pick it up before it exploded.

And then it exploded.

Upham had noticed Wade sitting in the grass. He was breathing slowly, looking up at the hill and the smoke coming out of the hole below the destroyed bunker.

"All right," Wade said softly. "All right . . ."

"Wade," Upham said, frightened. "Wade!"

"Wade?" Sarge asked, walking toward him. "Did you get hit?"

Miller and Mellish ran to join them. Reiben followed, leaving his rifle behind. Jackson ran over, holding his wounded arm. Everyone halted when they saw the terrible sight: their medic was sitting in the grass, looking down, astonished, at five bullet holes in his chest.

Chapter 12   The Prisoner

Wade had trouble breathing. Upham, shocked, said, "They're not supposed to shoot medics; they're not supposed to shoot medics."

Some of the men grabbed Wade's medical pack; others pulled open his shirt, revealing his terrible wounds. Then they laid him down. Everybody talked and shouted at the same time.

"Drugs," Miller said to Jackson, who was looking through Wade's medical pack. "Give me the drugs."

"He was helping *me*," Jackson said. "He was coming to help *me*."

"Press on it!" Sarge said, bending over the bleeding medic. "Put some pressure on it!"

"Help me, Upham!" Mellish shouted. "Help me. Use your hands."

Upham moved to Wade and helped. Jackson had lost his usual calm. "Oh, God! Oh, God!" he said.

"Drugs. Where are the drugs?" Miller said.

"Here!" Sarge called.

They poured some on Wade's wounds.

"Wade? Wade? Can you hear me?" Miller asked, bending over the medic.

Wade looked at them with a weak smile. "How does it look?" he asked. His voice was calm, but his body was shaking.

"You're fine," Miller said. "You'll be OK . . ."

Wade reached out and gripped Miller's left hand with surprising strength. "Don't lie to a doctor . . ."

Miller paused. "I don't know, Wade. It doesn't look very good, I guess."

The shaking stopped; the drugs were working. Wade tried to raise his head to see his wounds, but couldn't. "Am I . . . am I shot in the . . . spine?"

"I don't know," Miller admitted. Then he said to Sarge, "Here . . . lift him up a little . . ."

Sarge and Miller lifted the medic gently and carefully while Upham and Mellish kept pressure on the wounds.

"What . . . what do you see?" the medic asked.

Miller gently put his hand under Wade and touched his back—slowly and carefully. "The exit wound is on your spine," he reported. "At the bottom of your back."

Wade spoke with difficulty. "How . . . how big's . . . the hole?"

"The size of a small coin."

Wade sighed loudly. Miller withdrew his hand and laid Wade gently back on the grassy ground. The others kept pressing on the wound, but they couldn't stop the bleeding.

"I . . . can't move," Wade said, speaking very quietly.

"You're not dead, Wade!" Mellish insisted.

"Let me . . . let me feel . . ."

Wade tried to find his wounds, but he couldn't control his hand. "Help me . . ." Miller took the medic's wrist and guided his hand. "Is any place bleeding worse than the rest?"

"Upham and I are pressing on it," Mellish told him. "I don't think we should move our hands . . ."

"Show me . . . I have to feel . . ."

The other men guided their medic's hands to his chest as Mellish and Upham lifted theirs. Wade put his fingers down into the wound. The squad watched in horror—this was worse than anything they had seen in the past few days.

Then Wade's expression was not one of pain, but one of a sad child trying not to cry. "Oh, God . . . Oh, God . . ."

Upham, trying to seem calm, asked, "What should we do? You're a doctor! Tell us how to help you!"

Wade looked at Miller, his eyes sending a message that the captain easily understood: "*There's nothing you can do . . .*"

The medic took his hand away from his wound, and Mellish and Upham pressed down on it again.

Wade's voice was suddenly calm. He and Miller stared at each other. "I could use . . . some extra pills . . . to stop the pain."

Miller knew exactly what his friend was asking him to do. "Give me the pain pills," he said to Sarge.

Sarge obeyed, handing him some pills. Miller gave them to Wade, who took them and immediately asked for more.

"More," Miller said to Sarge.

"Sir, I . . ."

Everyone looked at Miller and Sarge.

"I said more."

"Yes, sir," Sarge said, handing Miller more pills, which he gave to Wade.

"Jackson . . ." Wade said.

"I'm here, Wade."

"Say a prayer . . ."

Jackson nodded and began to pray.

Mellish and Upham kept pressing on Wade's wounds. Jackson prayed aloud, and Wade smiled. Then Wade lifted his right arm, directing Miller's attention to something on the ground near his medical pack: the letter he had copied for Caparzo.

Miller looked at Wade and nodded. He picked up the letter, and Wade watched the captain put it into his pocket.

"I'll take care of it," Miller told him.

Wade smiled at his friend, Captain John H. Miller—Addley, Pennsylvania. Then he looked upward and said, "Mama . . . Mama . . ." And he died.

For a long time the soldiers didn't move; they just sat there and stared at their dead friend. No one spoke. They didn't blame Miller, whose order to take the machine gun had resulted in the medic's death. They didn't need to, because Miller knew it was his fault. His expression told his men how he felt.

Only Upham was crying. He had known Wade only two days, but he felt like he had lost a brother.

Suddenly they heard someone shout in German. Their heads turned quickly toward the field, across which a German soldier was walking toward them from the direction of the hill. His arms were raised, and blood was running down his face from under his flat helmet.

Reiben picked up a rifle, stood up, and ran toward the German, who stopped in terror. Reiben hit him in the face with the end of the rifle. The German fell, and Reiben began kicking him. Then Jackson and Mellish joined in the kicking.

"Was it you?" Mellish said. "Did you kill Wade? You *don't* kill medics, you garbage bag!"

Miller and Sarge watched from the grass, showing no emotion. They didn't stop the others.

"Let's shoot him . . ." Jackson said.

Mellish pointed his rifle in the German's face. "Do you have any last words, German, before we kill you?"

Reiben pulled the German to his feet. The others had their weapons ready to fire when Miller finally called out, "First make him cover up Wade for the burial squad."

They looked at Miller. They didn't want to stop, but he was their captain."

"Make him cover them, too," Miller said, pointing to the dead paratroopers in the grass.

The frightened German stood there—his eyes wide and wild, his hands in the air. Reiben just stared at the enemy soldier. He had nothing to say.

"Check him for weapons," Miller advised.

Staring at his prisoner, Reiben stood motionless.

"I'll do it, sir," Jackson said.

"Ask him one thing," Mellish said angrily. "Ask him if he killed Wade."

From the grass Sarge called out, "It doesn't matter. Wade's dead anyway."

Miller approached his sharpshooter, whose arm was still bleeding. "Jackson, are you OK?"

"The bullet made a small hole," Jackson said. "I'll be all right."

"Clean it and put a bandage on it. We're our own medics now."

"Yes, sir."

"Then you and I will be the guards. You watch the south; I'll watch the north."

The German spoke. Miller turned slowly and looked at him. He looked like he was ready to cry. He spoke again.

"Sir," Upham said, "he says—"

"I don't care what he says," Miller replied, walking past the German and into the field. "Reiben, come with me . . ."

Reiben walked with Miller while Upham, behind them, said, "Sir, you're not going to let them just kill this guy, are you?"

Miller said nothing.

"Sir—this isn't right, sir. There are rules . . ."

Miller didn't stop, but he looked back over his shoulder at Upham and said, "Help him with the bodies."

Miller and Reiben climbed the hill and entered the machine-gun hole. Two burned, bloody bodies lay across the gun and sand bags. In one corner there was an open soldier's pack.

"Check for maps," Miller said. "Any kind of information." Reiben said nothing. "Did you hear me, Private?"

The boy nodded, staring at the dead bodies. Then he joined Miller, who was looking through the contents of the pack. Miller found a wallet; inside were two photographs: one of a young boy holding a soccer ball and another of the same boy in uniform, standing with his proud, smiling parents. The smiling young soldier in the photo was their prisoner.

Near the bodies Reiben found a shopping bag from a store in Paris. Smiling, he reached inside and pulled out a pretty blouse. He stopped smiling, threw it on the ground, and walked out of the hole.

Miller, watching him go, said nothing. He stared at the photograph of their prisoner and his parents for several moments. Then he tore it into small pieces, threw them on the ground, and went out.

Beyond the hedges at the edge of a small field nearby, Upham was guarding the German prisoner as he covered the bodies with rocks. The corporal and the prisoner had dragged the nine bodies—the eight paratroopers and Wade—to this field. After the German covered each body, Upham put a rifle in each temporary grave, to tell the burial squads that these were American bodies.

Finally Upham told the prisoner to take a break, and they both sat on the ground. Upham began to smoke; the German watched him enviously. Upham gave him a cigarette.

"American cigarette," the German said. "I like American ... Mickey Mouse!"

Upham nodded seriously. They were still smoking when Miller walked into the field, followed by Sergeant Horvath and the rest of the squad: Reiben, Mellish, and Jackson.

"Make him stand up!" Mellish shouted angrily.

Upham stood and threw away his cigarette; the German copied his behavior.

Miller went from one rock-pile grave to the next. Upham had placed rifles there and Miller removed the bullets so the weapons couldn't be used. Pointing their rifles at the prisoner, Reiben, Mellish, and Jackson walked toward him and stood in a half circle around him. The prisoner looked at them anxiously and then began putting rocks on top of the next body.

He spoke in German, nodding to the rock-pile graves and working hard. He wanted to prove to the American soldiers that he was a good, obedient worker. He spoke again.

"He says he's not finished," Upham translated.

"That's what he thinks," Mellish said. Then he grabbed the prisoner by his shirt, and Jackson joined in.

The German pulled away from them, picked up a rock, and quickly began covering the last body. Reiben prepared to shoot. Hearing the sound of the rifle, the prisoner carefully stood up and turned to face the Americans.

"Please," he said in English. "I like America." His accent was bad, but he tried to smile.

Jackson prepared to shoot. Mellish prepared to shoot.

The prisoner stood straight now and sang, "Oh, say can you see . . ." That was all he knew of the American national song, but he sang it again and again.

The three privates were standing like a firing squad now—in a line, facing the prisoner. Feeling sick, Upham looked away. Miller and Sarge were still emptying the rifles. They seemed to be unaware of—or unconcerned about—what was happening.

The young prisoner tried again: "Kill Hitler!"

"Kill you!" Reiben said.

The prisoner jumped at Upham, grabbed his arm, and started shouting in German, extremely frightened.

Upham called to Miller, "Sir, he says he's sorry about Wade. I don't think he was the gunner, sir."

"Tell him that being sorry isn't enough," Jackson said, his rifle ready to kill.

"Tell him," Miller said, "the war's over for him."

The squad members nodded, and Miller walked over to the German. He took a handkerchief from one of his pockets and quickly tied it around the German's head, over his eyes.

"Sir," Upham said softly but urgently, "this isn't right."

"Just tell him, Corporal. Tell him what I said."

Upham did.

Miller turned the German around so that his back was to the squad. Horvath didn't want to, but he joined the others in line and prepared to shoot. The prisoner jumped.

Miller looked at his squad. Then he said to Upham, "Tell him to march 200 steps and wait until he can't hear us anymore. Then he must surrender to the first Americans he meets."

"What?" Reiben said, shaking his head. He couldn't believe what he had heard. "Wait a minute—"

"Yes, sir," Upham said, feeling better but not smiling. And he spoke in German to the young prisoner.

Miller checked the handkerchief, tying it a little tighter. Then he hit the German twice on the shoulder, signaling him to leave, which he did.

"You're letting him go?" Reiben asked Miller.

The German sang a popular American song as he walked away: "Take me out to the ball game! Take me out to the crowd! Buy me some peanuts . . ."

"All right," Miller said. "Everybody get your equipment and prepare to leave."

But nobody moved. Everybody was staring at him or watching the German as he walked toward the hedges across the field.

Miller sighed. "We can't take him with us. He'll make it difficult to complete our mission. In the direction I sent him, he'll get picked up by American soldiers."

"If he doesn't get picked up by German soldiers first," Reiben said angrily. "Then he'll be fighting again, and maybe he'll shoot another of us . . . You let the enemy go, sir. You just let him walk away."

Mellish watched the figure of the prisoner as it became smaller in the distance. "It's not right," he said.

"What's not right?" Upham shouted. "We don't kill prisoners! It's against the rules!"

"This isn't a game," Reiben shouted. "There *are* no rules!"

"Reiben," Miller said without expression, "get your equipment and stop talking."

Reiben didn't move. "No, sir. I don't think so . . . sir."

Everyone looked at Miller and Reiben. The German had disappeared beyond the hedges.

"That's not a suggestion, Reiben. It's an order."

"Really? Like the one you gave to take the machine gun? Because that order was a bad one, sir. Really bad."

Miller said nothing, but Horvath was extremely angry. "Soldier, you can't talk to your captain like that!"

Reiben ignored the sergeant, saying to Miller, "Yes, sir, Captain, that was a really bad order. We destroyed the machine gun, and we lost only one man doing it. Just our medic . . . Of course, with you in command, who needs a medic? We'll all be dead by sunset."

"Reiben . . ." Sarge said, moving toward the private.

But Reiben ignored Sarge's threat, saying to his captain, "If we lose more men, Ryan's mother will feel even better. She'll know how valuable her son's life was. The only problem is that we haven't found her son yet, but that's not important . . ."

Sarge was next to Reiben now, almost shouting, "Get in line, Private, and stop talking!"

Reiben turned around and walked away from them both— captain and sergeant.

Miller stood motionless, but Horvath, angrier than before, was shaking as he shouted loudly, "Don't you walk away from your captain!"

Jackson was staring at his rifle, thinking about what he and his friends had almost done. "Let him go . . . We don't need him."

Miller watched Reiben walk away. Suddenly Mellish was

73

beside him, looking him in the face and speaking desperately. "Listen, Captain, don't worry about Reiben. He's no good. I'll stay with you until we're finished. But listen to what I think: Ryan's dead. Dead in the grass, just like those paratroopers. I'm sure. We should just go back, sir."

Miller said nothing and moved away from the private. He saw a big rock, went to it, and sat down. His squad was coming apart.

"Reiben!" Sarge shouted to the departing figure, walking in the same direction as the German. The men didn't know if he was leaving his squad or following the German. "Get in line—now!"

His back to them, Reiben called, "No, sir. I'll go to prison if I have to. But I won't be part of *this* squad anymore."

"I'm not going to say it again," Sarge said, and the threat in his voice surprised all of them. He took his gun out. "*Get in line, soldier!*"

The sound of Sarge putting bullets in his gun scared Reiben, and he stopped walking. It got Miller's attention, too, but the captain remained seated—he couldn't make himself move.

Reiben turned and walked back toward the sergeant. His eyes were wide with fear and amazement and anger as he said, "You'd shoot *me* because of Ryan? You'd shoot me because of somebody we've never met?"

"Just get in line, soldier," Sarge repeated. He spoke more quietly now, but his gun was pointed at the returning Reiben.

"Good, do it, shoot me in the leg, please! Make it a good wound that will make the army send me home!"

"I'll shoot you on your lips," Sarge said, still pointing the weapon as Reiben came closer, "and make you stop talking!"

Reiben raised his hands over his head, saying, "Do it, Sarge! Do it!"

"Sarge," Mellish said, looking ready to cry, "put the gun away, please!"

But Sarge was extremely angry as Reiben walked toward him saying, "No, don't listen to them ... shoot me, Sarge! Then the Germans won't have to use their bullets."

Sarge's hand was shaking. Upham ran over to where Miller sat on his rock. The corporal urged, "Sir, *do* something!"

Miller just looked at Upham.

Reiben came closer to Sarge and the pointed gun.

"How much has been bet?" Miller asked Upham quietly.

"What?"

"You know—the bet about me. How much is there now?"

The corporal stared at the captain. He couldn't believe what he had heard. "I don't know."

Sarge shouted, "Stop right there!"

"Come on, Sarge! Put a bullet in my leg! Send me home!"

"You coward . . ."

Reiben stopped in front of Horvath and looked at the gun. "You're the coward! *Shoot* me! Make Ryan's mother happy!"

Upham, looking back at Reiben and Horvath, stood beside Miller. "Sir, I *really* think you need to do something about this—"

"I'm a high-school teacher," Miller said in a quiet but firm voice.

Mellish heard him and looked at him.

"I teach English," Miller said, sitting straight, "at Thomas Alva Edison High School."

Now Jackson looked at the captain. Sarge did, too. And Reiben.

"In Addley, Pennsylvania," Miller continued. "At home, when I tell people, they look at me and say, 'You look like a teacher.' But here ... I guess it's not as obvious ..." They were all staring at him. "You all look surprised, anyway."

They moved toward him, slowly, gathering around him.

"Maybe I've changed," he said softly. Then he laughed—just a little. "Sometimes I wonder if my wife would recognize me now."

Mellish turned to Jackson and whispered, "*Wife?*" Jackson's eyes were wide.

Slowly Miller stood up, sighing loudly. Then he said, "Look ... I don't know anything about Private James Ryan, and I don't care about him. The man's nothing to me. I just want to go home and see my kids."

Mellish looked at Jackson again, "*Kids?*"

"And if I can get closer to home by going to Ramelle and picking up Ryan," Miller continued, "then I'm going to Ramelle." He looked from face to face. "If any of you want to go back and fight the war in some other place, I won't stop you. I won't report you, either—if I survive. I'll say we got separated. Terrible things happen in a war ... I don't know anything anymore—except that I feel a very long way from home."

The wind whispered through the hedges, the high grass, and the leaves on the trees. The men stood silently listening to it, and thinking.

Finally Jackson said, "You're a *school*teacher?"

"That's right," Miller said.

"Caparzo knew," Upham said. "He told me he knew ... I think we should send the money from the bet to his parents."

"That's a good idea, Upham," Mellish said.

Reiben studied the captain. "Schoolteacher. You know, I joined the army to get away from people like you."

And Reiben grinned.

Miller grinned, too.

"I also coach the baseball team," Miller admitted.

Everybody was smiling now. They weren't happy—not in these circumstances—but they were pleased to feel like a squad again. Miller told Upham and Mellish to finish covering the last two paratrooper bodies with stones as the rest of the men got their equipment.

"Are we ready?" Sarge asked.

"We're ready, sir," Jackson said.

"All right, then," Sarge said. "Get in line."

The men got in line and moved out of the field.

"Our next stop," Reiben said, "is Ramelle."

Chapter 13   Ramelle

The afternoon sun was hot as the tired men walked through the tall grass. The land sloped gently to the Merderet River valley and Ramelle. Although they were only a kilometer away, the men couldn't see the river or the bridge that made Ramelle so important. But they could see the ruins of the village, which had been completely destroyed by American bombing. Only a few buildings and a church bell tower had survived.

"It looks quiet down there," Sarge commented from the front of the line. "There aren't any civilians in sight—and I don't see anyone from the 101st."

Miller responded from the back, "You'll see the paratroopers when we reach the bridge, but the citizens of Ramelle have probably left. It won't stay quiet much longer."

Suddenly they heard the sound of an engine behind them and turned their heads. The sound didn't surprise them because it was similar to the sound of farmers' tractors in the countryside. But the vehicle coming toward them was not a tractor. It was a German tank, moving quickly across the field with three groups of soldiers running along beside it.

The machine gunner on top of the tank began firing as the squad ran toward town as fast as they could. They jumped into a ditch, putting themselves below the bullets that hit the grass along the edge of the ditch.

On the other side of the ditch were railroad tracks, another ditch, and then the town. Miller realized that if he and his squad could get over the tracks, they would have good cover and a chance to fight. They ran across the ditch and were climbing up the other side when German bullets began hitting the tracks, forcing them back down.

Then the machine gun was silent.

"Now!" Miller shouted. "Shoot!"

They began firing back at the Germans, but there were so many bullets coming at them that they had to stay down. They fired over the edge, without seeing their target. But they heard the sound of the tank coming closer and closer . . .

"*Heads down!*" somebody shouted.

Miller and his men obeyed as they looked around at each other, wondering who had given that order. Then they realized that none of them had; it had come from behind them. Up on the railroad tracks they could see a huge gun pointing toward the field. They saw the flash of flame and smoke as a shell went over them. They heard the sound as it hit the tank and exploded. Looking over the edge of the ditch, they saw black smoke coming from the halted tank. The machine gunner had been blown apart.

The German foot soldiers had stopped, too. Suddenly four American paratroopers rose from the tall grass to the left of the ditch and began shooting their machine guns at the Germans. The sound of screaming filled the air as bullets hit them. Then there was silence.

With relief, the squad looked up behind them at a tall paratrooper kneeling on the train tracks, looking at them. He was a good-looking kid—blond with blue eyes and a serious face.

"Is everybody OK?" he asked. "Was anybody injured?"

"We're all OK. No injuries," Miller said. "Thanks for saving our lives. Who are you, son?"

"Private First Class Ryan, sir . . ." He saw the expression on Miller's face. "Sir? Is something wrong?"

The five American soldiers in the ditch were staring up at the man who had saved them with shocked expressions. Then they shook their heads and laughed. Private James F. Ryan—twenty, Peyton, Iowa—wondered if these men had gone completely crazy.

The squad climbed out of the ditch and onto the railroad tracks. This farm boy who had rescued them was not aware of their purpose here. They had to inform him that he had lost his brothers to this war.

Private Ryan and several other paratroopers accompanied Captain Miller and his squad through the ruins of Ramelle. There were no civilians in this town, and the paratroopers, Miller observed, looked the same as him and his men: tired, dirty, and occasionally wounded.

Miller and his men didn't say anything to Ryan yet. They glanced at him secretly—he looked like an Iowa farmer. But they respected him because he had saved their lives.

The Ramelle bridge over the Merderet was narrow—a brick and steel structure on a stone base. Below it, the Merderet was wide and blue. Both ends of the bridge were blocked with piles of sand bags that had machine guns on them. Corporal Fred Henderson—twenty-four, St. Louis, Missouri—came out from behind one of these piles. He smiled as he looked at the small group of tired soldiers walking toward him.

"If you're our assistance, I may have to complain," he said.

"I understand, Corporal," Miller said. "I need to report to your commanding officer."

"That would have been Colonel Jennings, sir." And the corporal nodded toward the river bank, where two dozen covered bodies waited for a burial squad. Then he said, "I'm afraid I'm the highest-ranking officer we have. Henderson, sir."

"I'm Captain Miller."

"Why did you come here, Captain?"

"We're here because of him," Miller said, pointing to Ryan. "We're looking for Private Ryan."

"Me?" Ryan said in amazement. "Why . . .?"

Miller was ready to finish this assignment. "James Francis Ryan? Iowa?"

"Yes, sir," Ryan said, confused and a little worried. "Peyton, Iowa, sir . . . What's this about?"

"There's no easy way to say this, soldier," Miller said, and paused briefly. "James, your brothers have all been killed in action."

"All of them?" Ryan asked. "Not all of them . . . there must be a mistake . . ."

"It's not a mistake, Private. Thomas died on Omaha Beach; Peter died on Utah Beach; Daniel died more than a week ago in New Guinea . . . I'm sorry, son."

The paratrooper said nothing. He thought about the boys he had grown up with—brothers he'd fought with and laughed with and sometimes hated and always loved. They were gone. He would never see them again. They had disappeared with Captain Miller's words.

Removing his helmet, Ryan walked over to the side of the bridge and leaned against it. Miller and his squad looked down at their feet, not watching as tears came down Ryan's cheeks. Ryan's paratrooper friends stared at the river.

Soon the private wiped the tears from his eyes, dried his hand on his pants, and looked toward Miller. "How far did you come to deliver this message?"

"We came from Omaha Beach."

He looked at them. "You came all that way—just to tell me this? Why? What's this really about, sir?"

Miller walked over to Ryan, who was still leaning against the bridge. "They're sending you home, son. We have orders to bring you back."

Ryan's eyes opened wide. "What do you mean, bring me back?"

"That's what our orders are. You're from Iowa. I don't have to tell you about the Sullivans."

Ryan smiled a little and said, "I understand—if I die, I'm bad publicity."

"Your mother has suffered enough of a loss ... You can have ten minutes to get your equipment and say goodbye to your friends."

Ryan was confused. Miller turned to Henderson and asked, "Is there any chance that assistance will reach you out here?"

"I don't know, sir."

"Do your radios work?"

"No, none of them work. We don't know what's happening south of us."

Then Ryan said, "I have orders, too, sir." The private wasn't leaning against the bridge anymore—he was beside Miller, standing straight. He spoke firmly. "And they don't include abandoning my position."

Miller sighed and said, "I understand how you feel. I'd feel the same way if I were you. But my orders have priority over yours."

"I don't agree, sir."

It had been a long day, and despite the sympathy he felt for this kid, Miller was getting angry. "Private, these orders come directly from General Marshall, Chief of Staff of the United States Army."

"With all respect, sir," Henderson interrupted boldly, "Private Ryan is right. General Marshall isn't here to judge the situation as it is now."

Miller frowned.

"Sir," Henderson said, "our orders are to keep control of this bridge—at all costs. Our planes have blown up every bridge across the Merderet except for two: one at Valognes and this one.

If the Germans take them, we'll lose our position and have to go back."

"I didn't come to take you and your men off this bridge, Corporal, or out of this town. I don't envy your job or doubt its importance, but you'll have to do it without this man."

Ryan was shaking his head, no. "I can't leave them, sir. Not until assistance arrives. There aren't enough of us now . . ."

"Private, you now have five minutes to get your equipment and report back to me."

Ryan was still shaking his head, no. "Captain, if I leave, what are they going to—"

"Hey, stupid!" Reiben interrupted angrily. "Two of us died trying to find you and get you home! You'd better come with us! I would."

The blood left Ryan's face. He looked at Miller for confirmation, and Miller nodded. Then he walked over to the sand bags and sat down.

"What . . . what were their names?" he asked quietly.

Mellish answered, "Wade and Caparzo."

Ryan repeated: "Wade . . . and . . . Caparzo."

The private repeated the names quietly to himself several times, trying to imagine these names as men—dead men. After a few minutes he said to Miller, "Sir, this doesn't make any sense. What have I done to deserve special treatment?"

Miller replied, "This isn't about you. It's about politics . . . and your mother."

But Ryan didn't seem to hear Miller. "I mean, my life isn't worth the lives of two others."

The men in Miller's squad looked at each other. They were confused and ashamed to hear Ryan express their own opinions.

The private gestured to the paratroopers around him. "These guys deserve to go home as much as I do—as much as anybody does. They've fought just as long and just as hard."

"Is that what I should tell your mother?" Miller asked. "Should I tell her that she can put another flag in her window?"

Ryan stared at Miller. "My mother didn't raise us to be cowards."

The captain stared at the private. "She didn't raise you to lose you."

"Well, then, you can tell her this. When you found me, I was with the only brothers I had left—the men in my squad. Tell her that I couldn't abandon those brothers. You tell her that ... and she'll understand."

And the private stared at the captain.

Miller said nothing.

"I'm not leaving this bridge, sir," Ryan said. "If you want to shoot me for not abandoning my position, do that ... although I'm not sure how you'll explain that to my mother."

Ryan moved past Miller and his men and went behind the sand bags. He stood there beside a machine gun—in his position, ready to fight.

Miller stared at the river.

"What are your orders, sir?" Sarge was at his side now. His face had no expression, but his eyes were bright.

Horvath had spoken softly, and Miller responded softly. This was a private conversation, and no one attempted to listen.

"Sergeant," Miller said, "it's difficult to decide what to do."

Horvath replied, "Yes, it is. But the question remains, sir: what are your orders? Should we arrest, and maybe shoot this man— the man General Marshall has ordered us to send home to his mother? We could wound him and carry him back with us; it wouldn't slow us down much. And who knows? Maybe we won't meet anymore Germans."

"What are you thinking, Sarge?"

Sarge smiled. "I'm not sure you really want to know, sir."

"Mike, I really do want to know."

Horvath hesitated, but the expression in Miller's eyes showed that he meant what he said.

"I don't know," Horvath sighed. "Part of me thinks the kid's right—he doesn't deserve special treatment, and he doesn't deserve to be taken from his position. That would just make things harder for his friends. He wants to stay here, so OK—let's leave him and go home."

"Part of you thinks that."

"Yes. The other part thinks ... what would happen if we stayed here and gave these guys the assistance that they need? And what would happen if we survived and left, and Private Ryan willingly went with us?"

"Yes?"

"If we did that, someday we might look back on this and think that we did the right thing. Saving Private Ryan was the one decent thing that we were able to do in this awful war."

Miller thought about that.

Sarge continued: "You said it yourself, Captain—maybe if we do that, we'll all earn the right to go home."

The captain sighed and smiled. "You know, for a minute ... I thought I was listening to Wade."

"Thanks, sir ... Anyway, those are my thoughts, sir."

Horvath walked away and rejoined the squad, giving Miller a few moments alone to think. They waited for his decision.

Then Miller walked slowly to Corporal Henderson, who stood near the sand bags. "What's your plan, Corporal?" he asked.

"My plan, sir?"

"How do you plan to prevent the Germans from crossing this bridge?"

Henderson gestured. "Well ... we have machine guns at both ends, as you can see ... and we mined the road through town ..."

Miller nodded, considering that. "Machine guns and mines

84

will slow them down—maybe for a minute. Have you done anything else?"

Henderson seemed embarrassed. "No, sir."

"How do you think the Germans are going to come? When they come to cross this bridge, they'll be coming with tanks."

"I know that, sir."

"Maybe your new commanding officer can think of something better."

Henderson frowned in confusion. "Who, sir?"

"Your new commanding officer," Miller said. "Me."

Chapter 14   The Bridge

Paratroopers Bill Trask—twenty-three, Dallas, Texas—and Ray Rice—twenty-two, Tulsa, Oklahoma—took Miller to the end of the bridge near Ramelle, where there was a pile of guns, mines, grenades, and bullets. Miller inspected the weapons. Sarge was at his side; the boys of the squad—and Ryan—were gathered behind them.

"Is this everything?" he asked.

"That's everything," Trask apologized. "It won't be much when the German tanks arrive."

Sarge looked at the small pile of weapons. "What do you think, Captain?"

"I think the Germans are going to destroy us."

"Yes," Sarge nodded.

Miller pointed. "What would happen if we could make some of them go down the main road . . . between those buildings? We can use the broken bricks and stones to make the passage narrower. Then they can't go through it."

Ryan said, "There aren't enough bricks and stones to stop a tank . . . unless we can stop one of the tanks . . ."

"Yes!" Miller said, grinning. "If we destroy a tank there, it'll block the road. Then we have a chance to fight them."

Nobody was grinning back at him. They wanted to share his enthusiasm, but they knew his suggestion would be difficult.

But Corporal Henderson was nodding, realizing the possibilities. "Yes . . . that would separate them. We can't let them all group together."

"Right," Miller said. "Then we could shoot at them one at a time—not in one big battle, but little battles that we can win. And as we do, we'll move back toward the bridge and fight the rest of them."

Sarge was nodding now and pointing along the road. "We can have a machine gun down here . . ." Then he pointed to the bell tower. "The second machine gun can go up there. It's high, and we can fire down on their heads."

"Good, good," Miller said. He turned to Jackson, "Do you want to operate the machine gun in that bell tower? From there, maybe you could kill a few German officers."

Jackson stretched his wounded arm and said, "I'm always glad to have a little time in church."

Miller slowly looked at the faces of his men. "What are your opinions?"

"You're asking us, sir?" Reiben said.

"Yes."

"Well . . . this isn't the worst idea I've heard."

Mellish said, "That's the truth! The worst idea was Omaha Beach."

They laughed and nodded; Miller smiled.

"The problem is that everything depends on making a tank go down the main street," Reiben said.

"That's right," Miller said. "And then destroying it."

"Well . . . how are we going to do that?"

"I hate to admit it, but Reiben's right this time," Sarge said, nodding toward the small pile of weapons. "How do we stop a tank with these? And how do we make a tank go where we want it to?"

"We'll give it something to chase," Miller said. "Then we'll hit it."

"What will we hit it with?" Reiben asked.

"Sticky bombs."

Now everyone—his squad, the paratroopers, and even Sarge—looked at Miller. Had he finally gone crazy?

"And what are sticky bombs, sir?" Reiben asked.

"Sticky bombs don't exist," Henderson said.

"They're in the army instruction manual," Miller said. "Look it up."

"We would, sir," Ryan said politely, "if we had one. Since we don't, maybe you could tell us."

"I'll be happy to. Do you have some explosives?"

"We have plenty of those," said Alan Toynbe—twenty-five, Malden, Massachusetts. "There are more than enough attached to the bridge."

"Then take some from there," Miller said, "to make the sticky bombs. This is how, boys: take one army sock, stuff it with explosives, and add a long piece of string. Then put grease all over the outside. It'll stick to anything you throw it at. That's a sticky bomb!"

They were still looking at him like he was crazy.

But soon Toynbe had a rope around him and was hanging from the side of the bridge, taking explosives from under it. He handed them to Trask and Rice, who were also hanging from the bridge. They passed them to Mellish and Upham on the bridge. Mellish and Upham delivered them to Miller, Ryan, Sarge, and several paratroopers, who manufactured the sticky bombs.

In the church, Jackson and paratrooper Ron Parker—twenty-one, Sommersville, Vermont—carried a machine gun, sniper's rifle, bullets, and other supplies up to the bell tower.

Two paratroopers were getting a machine gun ready behind a

pile of rocks down the street. Upham delivered bullets to them and moved on.

Inside a destroyed building, Private Mellish and Corporal Henderson were setting up the second machine gun. Upham delivered bullets to them, too.

"Upham," Mellish said, "listen to me. This is just the starting place. We'll move back toward the bridge, find new positions, and then move on again. You're going to have to find us and deliver the bullets quickly. Do you understand?"

Upham nodded. "I understand."

At the end of the bridge, the sticky bombs were ready. Miller, followed by the rest of the group from the bridge, walked through town, inspecting the battle preparations.

Private Ryan quietly asked the captain, "What's my position?"

"You stay close to me—never more than one step away. That's an order, Private. You still obey orders sometimes, don't you?"

With an embarrassed smile, Ryan quietly replied, "Yes, sir."

When he finished his inspection, Miller was satisfied that his men were positioned well. Then he—and Ryan—chose a place for two of them in what was left of the building nearest the bridge—a former café.

Miller was in position at the window; Ryan sat on a chair in the corner. He studied Miller for a while and then asked, "Is it true, what they say about you?"

"You'll have to tell me what you mean."

"Is it true that you're a schoolteacher?"

"Yes."

Ryan shook his head. "That's something I could never do. I know how my brothers and I acted in school. After that, I could never be a teacher."

Miller glanced at Ryan and saw the private's grief.

"I can't remember their faces. I keep trying, but I don't have any photos with me. I can't picture them in my head."

"You have to think of them in a situation."

"What do you mean, sir?"

"Don't try to think of their faces. Try to remember something you did with them. When I want to think about home, I think about lying in my backyard or about my wife working in her garden. When I do that, I'm there with them."

Ryan thought about this advice. Then he smiled, and reported to Miller: "One night, after dark, Tom and Pete dragged me out of bed, saying they had something to show me in the barn. Something really special. We went upstairs and looked down. Danny was there kissing a blonde girl. Then she heard something, looked up, and saw us looking down at her. She screamed and ran out fast. Danny was so angry that he chased us and ran into a candle. The candle fell over and started a fire. He had to stop chasing us and help us put out the fire before the whole barn burned down."

Miller smiled.

"Danny went to army training the next day," Ryan said. "That was the last time the four of us were all together—two years ago."

Miller nodded and smiled. They looked out the window, listening to the silence and enjoying their memories.

Then Miller heard something and stopped smiling. "Here they come," he said. "Here they come."

All around the ruins of Ramelle, and on the bridge, the men heard the engines of the approaching tanks—a sound they greeted with relief and horror. They prepared their weapons for battle.

Miller looked out at Jackson in the bell tower. Jackson was looking out to see what was approaching. Parker signaled with his fingers—four tanks, two of them Tigers and two Panzers.

The ground began to shake as the tanks came nearer. Then the first huge tank—a Tiger—came into view. Riding on top, the commander surveyed the village. Another Tiger followed the first, and the two smaller Panzers were behind it. Marching soldiers—about 100 of them—followed the tanks.

"God, give me strength," Jackson said as he looked down at the line of tanks and soldiers.

Miller said, "We're lucky. They're coming down the main street . . ."

He waited for the tanks to reach the blocked passage; Toynbe watched him. At Miller's signal he pulled the switch and exploded the buried mines. A dozen Germans were killed, and the others ran for cover. The Americans began firing their machine guns, killing and wounding more German soldiers.

Reiben and five paratroopers were hidden on both sides of the main street. When the first tank approached their position, they raced out, carrying their sticky bombs. They threw them at the tank's wheels and ran away, finding piles of broken bricks and stones to hide behind. The sticky bombs exploded in a cloud of black smoke. But the tank continued.

Then its wheels exploded, and the tank stopped, blocking the road, as Miller had planned. The other tanks stopped behind it, but the four tanks continued to fight. The machine guns on top of each tank turned and fired toward the Americans' hiding places. Americans around the village ran behind stone piles, diving for cover.

The German foot soldiers dragged their wounded off the street and ran for shelter. Then they, too, began to shoot back at the Americans.

From behind his rock pile, Sarge shot at the third tank, but his shell hit the tank and then exploded against the wall behind it. The wall fell. The tank's machine gun shot in Sarge's direction, and he ran.

From his position, Reiben watched this happen and saw smoke and flames coming from behind Sarge. When the smoke cleared, there was no sign of Sarge. He didn't know if Horvath was alive or dead.

The tanks left the main street and moved forward toward the bridge on other streets. Seeing this, Miller shouted to Ryan and Toynbe, "Let's go!"

Although the Americans had killed a lot of Germans, the numbers of the enemy were still a threat to the small group. In the church bell tower, Parker and Jackson, who never missed his target, shot at the Germans. Then bullets hit the tower. The two men looked at each other.

"Those Germans on the ground know we're here now," Parker said. "I hope they don't tell their friends on the tanks."

One of the smaller tanks hit a stone wall and tried unsuccessfully to push through it. Miller saw this and sent two paratroopers to attack it. They raced out, sticky bombs in their hands, toward the struggling Panzer.

Private Ryan began to follow them, but Miller grabbed his arm, saying, "Not you."

Then the Germans approached. The captain and the private began shooting to provide cover for the two runners. The two paratroopers reached the tank and paused to get their sticky bombs ready to throw. One went off early, killing the two soldiers. It also hit the wall, which broke apart, making it possible for the Panzer to move ahead.

The American machine gunners moved to new positions, and Upham ran from one team to the other, delivering more bullets. The American and German foot soldiers continued firing at each other. And the tanks kept moving down the streets—going through walls, firing, destroying anything in their paths.

The second Panzer reached Reiben and Toynbe's position. They ran out and attacked it, putting sticky bombs on its wheels and running away quickly. Reiben was thrown to the ground when the bombs exploded. But the tank went on—undamaged!

It turned toward Reiben, who climbed desperately on the rocks to get out of the Panzer's path. From his new position, Reiben couldn't see that the tank had been hit, but he heard it halt. He glanced back at the motionless tank and also saw Sarge sitting on top of a pile of rocks nearby. The two men looked at each other. Sarge smiled and ran out of sight behind a half-wall.

Glad to see Sarge alive, Reiben looked back at the tank. At that moment, a man in the Panzer stood up and shot Toynbe. He was turning his gun toward Reiben when a bullet hit him in the chest, killing him.

Surprised, Reiben turned and looked up, knowing that the shot had come from the bell tower—knowing that Jackson had saved him. Like Sarge had saved him . . . In those few seconds, his life had been saved twice by two of his brothers . . .

In the bell tower, Jackson, praying, was already searching for more targets.

Reiben led a group of paratroopers to attack the damaged Panzer. A second German came out of it. Reiben shot him and then joined the others, who were throwing grenades into the tank. They raced away as it exploded behind them.

Jackson looked through his gun's special attachment at the disabled Tiger, which still blocked the main street. Its gun was raised, pointing at the bell tower. "Parker! Get out of here—now!" Jackson shouted. The two men raced to the door, but they both knew they wouldn't reach it. Just then the tower exploded.

From their machine-gun position, Mellish and Henderson watched as the tower was destroyed.

"Jackson!" Mellish shouted, staring in horror.

"We have to destroy that Tiger," Henderson said. He took out a grenade.

"Are you crazy? That's a Tiger! Grenades don't destroy Tigers!"

Henderson grinned and raced into the street. Mellish fired his machine gun, giving Henderson the cover he needed to get close to the tank. Henderson, grenade ready, waited until the machine gun stopped firing. Then he ran straight to the tank, jumped up, and threw the grenade at the gun. He got out a second grenade, prepared it, and waited for the tank to stop shaking from the explosion. Then he climbed onto the tank, and threw his grenade into it.

The explosion threw Henderson onto the street. He stood up, grinning, and ran back toward Mellish, shouting excitedly, "Did you see that?"

And from somewhere, German machine-gun fire hit him. Mellish screamed and kept firing and screaming and firing until he had no more bullets. But the Germans still had bullets, and they were hitting all around Mellish. He grabbed his gun and ran.

Changing positions, Miller ran—with Ryan following him—and took cover behind a wall. Sarge was already there, firing at the Tiger as it moved toward them.

"Go to the meeting place! Run!" Miller shouted. The men left just as the Tiger crashed through the wall.

Mellish, running, saw Upham ahead, confused in the smoke and dust. "Upham!" he shouted, and Upham looked back at him. "The bridge is straight ahead! Run!"

Just then, a young German soldier ran out of the smoke into Mellish's path. Both men were surprised and looked at each other for a second—both ready to fire. But the German was faster.

"Mellish!" Upham screamed.

And the German turned toward Upham, who stood motionless. The corporal knew that he was going to die. But suddenly three bullets hit the German's chest and threw him onto a pile of stones. He lay there, staring.

Upham was shocked to be alive. Reiben appeared next to the corporal, saying, "Come on, Upham, we have to go back." But

Upham didn't move, so Reiben dragged him to their meeting place near the bridge.

Miller, Ryan, and Sarge, ran for the meeting place, too. They could hear the Tiger nearby—destroying everything in its path.

From his position, Trask threw a grenade at the Tiger, but nothing happened. He ran for the meeting place, too.

Miller, Ryan, Sarge, Trask, Reiben, and Upham arrived at the same time. Then they raced for the sand bags on the bridge and dove over. They got to safety just as machine-gun fire hit the sand bags.

The remaining Panzer joined the Tiger, and both tanks moved toward the bridge and its defenders. The remaining German foot soldiers walked beside them.

Ryan picked up a huge gun. Miller put bullets in it and told Ryan to fire. He did.

"Reiben and I will take this gun," Sarge told Ryan. He looked at Miller, reminding him of their real mission. "You two go to the other end of the bridge!"

Miller nodded, grabbing Ryan's arm. He said to Horvath, "You can't keep this position much longer—follow right behind us!"

Ryan and Miller grabbed all the weapons they could and ran across the bridge. Sarge and Reiben continued shooting at the Tiger, but the tank kept coming nearer. Upham and Trask fired at the German soldiers, occasionally hitting some.

The Tiger and Panzer came nearer and nearer.

Sarge shouted, "Let's go!" He and Reiben grabbed everything they could and ran.

One of the paratroopers stayed at the sand bags, firing to provide cover as the others ran across the bridge. When he saw the Tiger turn its gun toward his position, he jumped up and ran after Sarge and the others. Just then an explosion blew the sand bags apart and killed him.

Miller and Ryan reached the sand bags at the other end and

threw themselves over. The captain grabbed a huge gun, shouting to Ryan, "We can't let the Germans take this bridge!"

They got the gun ready to shoot.

Then Sarge, Reiben, Trask, and Upham ran out from the smoke on the bridge. The tank was right behind them.

"Run! Run!" Miller shouted.

The tank's machine gun fired at the runners, hitting Trask in the leg. Sarge picked him up and carried him behind a stone column on the bridge. The firing continued, and smoke provided temporary cover.

Sarge called to Reiben and Upham, "Go! Go!"

They joined Sarge, helping him drag Trask to a safer place.

Then the tank's machine gun fired again. Two bullets hit Sarge in his back, and he fell to the ground.

"Sarge!" Reiben screamed.

Miller aimed his gun again. "Get down! Get down!"

Reiben and Upham threw themselves down next to Sarge and the wounded Trask, and Miller fired over their heads at the tank. The noise and smoke of the explosion provided cover, which encouraged Reiben and Upham to get up. Reiben dragged Sarge, and Upham dragged Trask, and they slowly moved toward the sand bags.

The Tiger continued to move forward and shoot. Reiben and Upham, with Sarge and Trask, took cover behind a column.

The tank moved forward toward Miller and Ryan's position. They picked up a machine gun and put it on top of the sand bags. Ryan fired at the tank, which continued moving forward. Its gun was aimed at them. Then Miller remembered their mission. Thinking only of saving Private Ryan now, he put his arms over the boy and pushed him down out of the path of the bullets.

Those bullets missed Miller, but one of the German soldiers running beside the tank shot at them. His bullets hit Miller in the chest.

Both Miller and Ryan were out of sight now, but Upham had seen the shooting. And he had recognized the German who shot the captain.

And the corporal, who would one day write a book about these events, stepped out from behind the column, his gun ready. He looked at the German soldier, the young prisoner who liked Mickey Mouse and who Miller had allowed to live.

That soldier—that former prisoner—had not recognized the man he shot. But Upham was closer, and the German recognized him. "Upham!" he said, grinning and lowering his weapon.

Upham shot him through the heart.

As Upham and Reiben continued moving toward the sand bags, the wounded Miller sat up, took out his hand gun, and began firing at the tank. He shot his last bullets at the approaching Tiger, and the tank exploded. Astonished, he stared at his gun, wondering how his bullets could explode a tank.

Then there was a second explosion, and the tank went over the side of the bridge into the river. Miller heard the splash and another sound that made him look upward. In the sky he saw an American plane and knew that his gun had not destroyed the tank.

Reiben and Upham watched the plane from behind the column. The remaining Panzer and German foot soldiers were going back, desperate to get off the bridge. Not threatened by the tank now, the two men left Trask and Sarge's body and ran to their captain. Miller was lying in Ryan's arms.

"Captain," Reiben said. "Oh, God . . . Captain." He screamed curses and prayers. Upham cried. Ryan cried, too.

At the other end of the bridge, the smaller tank exploded. Miller tried to talk, but he couldn't. He raised his trembling hand and pointed to the planes.

Behind the soldiers on the bridge, American tanks came out from the trees and approached, accompanied by foot soldiers. But

Miller wasn't aware of them. He saw only the sky and the plane and the clouds.

Then he looked at Private Ryan, the man they had come to save—the man they had saved. "Earn this," he said softly.

"Sir?" Ryan asked.

The captain repeated it firmly, as an order: "Earn this."

His last words. His hand stopped shaking.

Ryan, Reiben, and Upham carried Captain John H. Miller away from the sand bags to the stone wall of the bridge and laid him gently there.

Reiben leaned over the captain and reached into his pocket, removing something and putting it in his own pocket. He didn't say anything, but Upham saw what Reiben had done. He knew Reiben would deliver the letter to Caparzo's father.

And Captain Miller's boys went back to the war.

PART FIVE ST. LAURENT MILITARY GRAVEYARD
JUNE 6, 1998

Chapter 15   Memories

James Ryan—seventy-four, Peyton, Iowa—walked through the perfectly lined rows of crosses until he found the right name. He walked so quickly that none of his family—not even his little grandson—could stay with him. And that was fine, because he wanted a private moment—a moment between private and captain.

He looked at the white cross and said, "My family's with me today. They wanted to come on their vacation. But I didn't know how I'd feel about coming back here."

"Grandpa!" Jimmy was almost with his grandfather.

Ryan continued to speak to his captain. "I think about what happened on that bridge every day. I think about what we did, and what you said to me. And I just want you to know . . ."

"Grandpa!"

Ryan turned and saw that Jimmy had stopped a short distance away. The grandfather gestured to his grandson to stay back, please, for just a short time.

Then Ryan looked at the cross and talked to it as if it were a person. "I've tried to live my life the best I could. I hope that's enough. I didn't invent anything. I didn't cure any diseases. I had a farm. I raised a family. I lived a life. I only hope that, in your opinion, I earned what you did for me."

"Jim . . ."

Now it was his wife's voice, not his grandson's. His son, his son's wife, and the four grandchildren had stopped a respectful distance away. Their expressions were confused; they didn't understand what this place meant to him.

But the woman he had lived with—this woman who stood beside him now and always—understood. He had never really told her anything about this place—no war stories, except a few funny ones. But this was the woman who had held him and given him comfort on those nights—once frequent but now occasional—when he woke up screaming or crying or both.

She held his arm and looked down at the white cross. "Is it someone you knew?"

Ryan sighed. "Not really."

"Are you all right, Jim?"

He looked at her, and the tears in his eyes brought tears to hers. "Alice . . . have I lived a good life? Am I a good man?"

"Jim . . . what . . . ?"

"Just tell me . . . tell me if you think I've earned it."

She studied him and then touched his face. "Oh, yes. Yes, you have."

Then she left him there and joined the family, giving him more time alone.

After a last respectful look at the grave, Private James Ryan, winner of the Silver Star military honor, joined his family again. They left the cemetery behind . . .

And they left behind the grave of Captain John H. Miller, who had been given the highest military honor after his death.

In Addley, Pennsylvania, a junior high school was named after him. And in spite of a special sign in the school's front hallway, many of today's students wonder why.

ACTIVITIES

Chapters 1–4

Before you read

1　Have you seen or heard about the movie, *Saving Private Ryan*? What do you know about it?

2　Find the words in *italics* in your dictionary. They are all in the story. Match each word with a word below. What is the connection?

bunker　casualty　cliff　command　company　helmet　jeep medic　sharpshooter　trench

a	head	**b**	rifle	**c**	driver	**d**	medicine
e	officer	**f**	dig	**g**	group	**h**	shelter
i	earthquake	**j**	climber				

3　Find these words in your dictionary.

artillery　corporal　cover　explosive　grenade　lieutenant machine gun　mine　mortar　private　shell

Which are words for

a　people in the army?

b　weapons?

c　a place where you are protected from weapons?

After you read

4　What do those sentences tell us about Captain Miller?

a　Then the captain moved among his boys, keeping his manner and his voice conversational and calm.

b　Then he dragged Delancey to the open gate and, still holding onto him, jumped into the deep water.

c　Miller ran into the open area and stood there, making a perfect target.

d　... he led his boys out from behind the rock pile and up the steep slope.

5　Answer the questions.

a　Who prays?

b　Who ignores orders and stays to help his friend?

c　Who is Miller's friend?

Chapters 5–6

Before you read

6 Put these in order of their rank in the army. Check the words in *italics* in your dictionary.

captain   *colonel*   corporal   *general*   lieutenant
private   sergeant

7 Find these words in your dictionary. Complete the sentences.

mission   parachute   paratrooper   squad

a After jumping out of the plane, she opened her . . . . . and floated safely to the ground.

b After the football game, the cleaning . . . . . will pick up the trash.

c Their . . . . . was to deliver medical supplies to the town after the earthquake.

d The . . . . . jumped out of the plane and landed in a tree.

8 In the next chapter, officers at the Pentagon, in Washington, DC, hear about a problem. What do you think the problem is?

After you read

9 Who says

a "I'd shoot myself before I even got off the boat."

b "If things hadn't been so terrible on the beach, we'd probably be in Caen right now."

c "If you live through this, you'll have some good stories to tell."

d "It isn't going to be easy, trying to find one soldier in the middle of this big war."

e "I'm writing a book."

10 Why does Miller say that their new assignment is a public-relations mission?

11 Do you think Upham will be a good addition to the squad? Why (not)?

Chapters 7–9

Before you read

12 Find the words in *italics* in your dictionary. Answer the questions.

a Are you a *civilian*?

102

b Who wears *dog tags*? Why?

c What does a *sniper* do?

After you read

13 Who

    a knows where the Captain is from?

    b knows about methods of attack?

    c has been in battles with Miller before?

    d kills the German sniper?

    e takes Caparzo's letter?

    f thinks more of the squad will be killed?

    g would not trade ten Ryans for one Caparzo?

14 Miller suggests that, "If you do the math, you can choose the mission over the men—every time." What is your opinion?

Chapters 10–12

Before you read

15 While the men walk "out into the night and the waiting war," they will talk. What do you think they will talk about?

After you read

16 How has Reiben's attitude toward the Japanese changed? Why? What do you think?

17 Complete the sentences.

    a Reiben thinks all Germans are . . . . . .

    b Upham feels like he lost . . . . . .

    c Miller says that their goal is . . . . . .

    d Wade believes that killing a man is . . . . . . It doesn't matter . . . . . .

    e Jackson's opinion of the German is that being sorry isn't . . . . . .

18 What are two of the decisions Miller makes? What would you have done in his place?

Chapters 13–15

Before you read

19 Who do you think will be alive at the end of the story?

After you read

20 Were you surprised by Upham's behavior during the fighting at Ramelle? Why (not)?

21 Did Private Ryan "earn this"? What do you think?

Writing

22 Upham says that fighting in a war should make men feel like brothers. Does this story support that statement or not? Explain, using examples.

23 Is it morally right to risk eight lives to save one? Why (not)? What do you think?

24 How does Reiben change his attitude and behavior between Omaha Beach and the Ramelle Bridge? Why do you think he changes?

25 You are Reiben, Upham, or Ryan. Write a letter to the parents of one of the men who died. Tell them how he died and express your feelings.

26 Which of the nine men—the eight in the squad and Ryan—do you like best? Explain why, giving examples of their speech and actions.

27 Choose three adjectives to describe Miller, and explain your choices.

Answers for the Activities in this book are available from your local office or alternatively write to: Penguin Readers Marketing Department, Pearson Education, Edinburgh Gate, Harlow, Essex CM20 2JE.